JEFF SMITH

Management Accounts Made Easy

The ultimate guide to understanding the financial information of the Automotive Industry.

YOURS TO HAVE AND TO HOLD BUT NOT TO COPY

Warning; photocopying this book will seriously damage your wealth.

Published by:
Insight Training & Development Limited
P. O. Box 1234
Stourbridge
England
DY8 2GE

Telephone: 0044 (0)1384 371432
Web Address www.AskInsight.com
Blog www.Jeff-Smith.com
Email: JeffSmith@AskInsight.com

Dedicated to my three girls.
Sharon, Sophie and Lara

I love you more than anything.
(and you can't beat that!)
(and you can't say the same!)

...and to Max, you're growing on me

About The Author

Jeff Smith is a #1 Best-Selling Author, Business Strategist and Motivational Speaker who's made several programmes for Sky Television He's particularly well known for his ability to explain and convey complex information into jargon-busting, plain English so everyone understands.

His client list reads like a "who's who" of global success and includes nothing less than Royalty, a string of Fortune 100 companies and with book sales in excess of $3,000,000, he's regarded as one of the very best business improvement strategists in the world.

As a Motivational Speaker, Jeff speaks at conferences all over the world sharing the 7 big secrets of the world's top achievers, focussing on how they use the most important Key Performance Indicators (KPI) so that you discover how to make more profit and keep it. If you would like to book Jeff for your conference, you can contact him using the details below:

☎ 0044 1384 371432

Email: jeffsmith@askinsight.com

Web Site: www.Jeff-Smith.com

Acknowledgments

When I first had the notion to write this book, I really wasn't sure whether it would be a viable proposition or not. To test the waters, I collated my thoughts and asked a few people if they thought the book would contribute any real value to the Automotive Industry. The responses I received are responsible for putting this book in your hands.

Whilst writing, I've worked with all manner of businesses including small independent Bodyshops with cash flow problems to large franchised dealerships, new vehicle manufacturers with world-wide franchised dealer networks, huge companies in the Middle East, Scandinavia and Europe and the largest PLC's in the Automotive Industry. From the largest companies in the world to the smallest, they all have one thing in common... they all use Management Accounts.

Unfortunately, this is where the problems begin because different people have different opinions about how Management Accounts should be structured and the industry has ended up with a myriad of different expressions and a multitude of confusing terminology.

My aim in writing this book is to cut through all of this confusion and incompatibility to bring together a central point of reference that suits the specific requirements of the Automotive Industry. I've looked at Management Accounts with the *sole purpose* of structuring them so that it is possible to understand what is happening at an operational level within

Sales, Service Parts and Bodyshop. If Management Accounts do not provide this vision, they are rendered worthless to the Managers who need to interpret them in order to grow their businesses.

With this principle as my guiding light, I've not been concerned with which accounting structures are "right or wrong" but rather which accounting structures are the most *useful* for the Managers of the Automotive Industry to derive commercial gain in the workplace.

During my many years of working as a Consultant with thousands of people, I've captured all of the best accounting practices and put them in this book for you. The terminologies, systems and processes are universal, they have always existed and I do not take credit for any them. All I have done is to collate the information, put it in one place and attempted to put it in a way that is most useful to understand operational performance.

I feel incredibly privileged that so many people have opened the doors of their companies, welcomed me in with open arms and provided so much confidential information so that this book contains all of the terminology that exists in the different manufacturers' vocabularies throughout the Automotive Industry. Once again, I've been fortunate enough to have been able to stand on the shoulders of giants.

There are many people, who over the past 30 years, have contributed greatly to my knowledge, sadly far too many to mention in this text, but you know who you are and I thank you for your generosity, support and patience.

On a personal note, this book was written during a difficult time in my family life and there are a few people I wish to thank who have provided me with the necessary motivation and inspiration to carry on writing. Some of these people will have no idea how much help and support they have given me at a time when I needed it most. The sincere kindness and thoughts that have been communicated in the occasional email and telephone call to see how things are going, business lunches that were arranged as a ruse to lift my spirits, the sincere handshakes with that little extra squeeze that conveyed much more than a simple hello or goodbye and the beautiful flowers that have been sent to my wife, all of these gestures have touched me deeply.

My sincere thanks go to Paul Maryan, Paul Stroud, Khalid Shaa'ban, Frank Lord, Wayne Edwards, Mark Burrows and Nick Tame. Whether you realise it or not, you have all had a part to play in the creation of this book. And also to my special friend and mentor, RAB Lee, who sadly lost his life at the age of 53. He was always 100% honest about my work kept me grounded; I miss this guy so much.

My special thanks and eternal gratitude go to my gorgeous wife, Sharon and my two beautiful daughters, Sophie and Lara. In the final stages of writing this book, I've been stressed out, moody, unbearable to live with and you have paid the price of my solitude. Thank you for your unerring support, I love you more than anything.

Thank you

How To Use This Book

This book is written for Managers and Accountants with different levels of knowledge and experience. Its aim is to achieve a meeting of minds to create a uniformed approach to the reporting of financial information within the Motor Industry. It's perfectly suited for the small independent business owner with a single workshop or used vehicle operation, right up to a major franchise with a fully fledged dealer network consisting of major groups and public limited companies.

It draws upon information gleaned from best practices across the globe ranging from the market extremes of the Middle East to Scandinavia and everywhere in between. In some sections, it provides clear guidance for Accountants so that the Management Accounts are structured to properly reflect operational performance in the workplace. In other sections it provides Managers with clear insight how to interpret Management Accounts correctly so that performance gains can be identified and delivered.

Beginning from the ground floor and working up, it travels all the way through the Management Accounts of the Motor Industry so that you can use the book to read all the way through as you might do with a novel, or you can simply use it as a reference guide at a time when you need a fast answer.

However, it is recommended that any people who are new to Management Accounts should read this book right from the beginning so that the foundations are firmly in place.

PART 1
THE PRINCIPLES OF MANAGEMENT ACCOUNTS

This section is written for the new and aspiring departmental Manager who requires an introduction to Management Accounts and how to interpret them. It covers the different terminology that's in use for profit and expenses including the terms Variable, Semi-Fixed, Direct, Indirect, Overheads, Direct Profit, Net Profit Before Interest and Net Profit. There's also chapter on how to interpret Management Accounts and an introduction to a manufacturers Composite.

PART 2
UNDERSTANDING THE DEPARTMENTS

This section bridges the gap between financial awareness and commercial awareness by providing guidance for Accountants to code the Nominal Ledger with clear and objective reasoning so that operational performance is highly visible. It also provides guidance for Managers to interpret each of the departments including Sales, Service, Parts and the Bodyshop.

PART 3
UNDERSTANDING THE BALANCE SHEET

Essential reading for everyone who owns this book. It's written as an introduction to the Balance Sheet and explains Working Capital and how much is required to run your business. It also explains how to fund a company correctly so that it does not go bust in turbulent times.

"If you have a great idea,
but you can't explain it to others,
you can't make a positive change in the workplace.

***Clarity is Power**."*

- Jeff Smith

Contents

Introduction

"We cannot solve our problems with the same thinking we used when we created them."

- Albert Einstein

INTRODUCTION

According to the Chartered Institute of Management Accountants (CIMA), Management Accounting is defined as:

> *"The process of identification, measurement, accumulation, analysis, preparation, interpretation and communication of information used by management to plan, evaluate and control within an entity and to assure appropriate use of and accountability for its resources."*

Now let's talk in plain English to understand what this means for the people of the Motor Industry.

The retail Motor Industry produces Management Accounts that are intricately detailed and extremely comprehensive in their final form. It's fair to say that the management information produced by the Motor Industry is, in many cases, far superior to many other industries.

This advantage has not happened by accident, it's happened by design because it's becoming more and more critical to measure the numerous activities that are conducted in a modern-day business, purely for means of survival. The good old days of high profitability and an abundance of cash flow have long since gone. The funding requirements within the Motor Industry are colossal and it is therefore vital to maximise the use of those funds to ensure that the business is operated with optimum efficiency so that it is able to grow and develop in forthcoming years. To do this, the whole management team must be fully conversant with Management Accounts and in total control of their business.

Management Accounts illustrate business direction, skills, ability and results, but the problem is that they can appear to be over complicated, daunting and downright confusing to anyone just starting out in a management position. To add to the confusion of the new Manager, different Accountants have different ways of doing things and Management Accounts in the Motor Industry produce a variety of different results. Different words and phrases are used with jargon and terminology that sounds like a foreign language, which makes the journey of understanding, a difficult and turbulent experience.

One of the problems creating this confusion is that the Motor Industry is unique in its approach to management development; there's rarely any career development *prior* to doing a new job. All too often, people are promoted into management positions without being given the necessary training to do the new job and they are left to their own devices.

Experience and success is to be gained by experimenting with trial and error mechanisms or from getting advice from the previous boss who learned the trade in exactly the same way. As a business strategy, it's really quite bizarre when you think about the huge responsibilities in business, staff welfare and the money that's involved in stocks and company resources.

Climbing The Corporate Ladder

The route to becoming a Dealer Principal in a franchised dealership and being at the helm of a business that produces multi-millions in revenues can be rapid and what's frightening is that it can be achieved without possessing an adequate amount of business acumen. This is not to decry the achievements of any Dealer Principals or any other Managers for that matter; it's simply a fact that exists within the culture of the modern-day franchised dealership. There are exceptions to every rule of course, but let's consider the generally accepted route to success in a franchised dealership.

It's true to say that a very high percentage of Dealer Principals in the Motor Industry began their career as a Sales Person. It's highly likely that they possessed good rapport skills, plenty of charisma and therefore sold a lot of cars, bikes, trucks or Power Equipment. All too often, the best Salesperson gets promoted to be the Sales Manager; not always a good decision.

Now in their first management position, the new Sales Manager knows how to value part-exchanges, sell vehicles, fill in order forms and produce invoices, but the problem is that no one has taught them anything about Sales Management yet and they're right in at the deep end; "sink or swim" are usually the words given in their induction to the new role.

The new Sales Manager is given a set of Management Accounts and panic sets in. After a while, some of the information can be deciphered, but the rest is a mystery so the Management Accounts are placed in the desk drawer, out of sight, out of mind.

The Sales Manager continues to motivate the Sales Team because they have targets to achieve and the job is all about making profit, keeping stocks looking good and to keep the manufacturer happy. The Sales Manager believes that it is this activity that gets measured and the figures in the Management Accounts are for the Accountant to study.

Occasionally, the Sales Manager retrieves the Management Accounts from the desk drawer to take another look, but the confusion is still in abundance so after plucking up the courage, a trip to the Accounts Team is in order to ask a few questions.

The Sales Manager asks a question and the answer is given by a member of the Accounts Team, but nothing computes. The Sales Manager's eyes glaze over, brains turn to mush because the explanation given is full of alien words which mean absolutely nothing whatsoever. The Sales Manager stands there for a moment, pondering in a state of even deeper confusion and then leaves the Accounts office with feelings of either incompetence or antagonism.

However, determination and the desire to succeed kicks into overdrive and the Sales Manager gets on with the task of selling more vehicles and hitting target. After a couple of years, despite the lack of any in-depth understanding of Management Accounts, credibility in the role is established as a consistent high performer and the manufacturer is in favour, so what happens next? The Sales Manager gets promoted to the role of Dealer Principal.

This is where the really serious fun begins because now the newly promoted Dealer Principal is given a full set of Management Accounts every month which not only has the Sales Department figures that are just about beginning to be understood, but they also contain the figures for the Service Department, Parts Department, Bodyshop, a full page of Company Overheads and a thing on the back called a Balance Sheet. Then to make matters worse, the manufacturer sends a copy of the franchise Composite, which is a set of statistics that looks even more complicated than the dealer Management Accounts.

The new Dealer Principal realises that there's a long way to go on this journey of understanding financial information. Discussions with the Accounts Team are more frequent and confidence ebbs and flows as feelings of confidence and frustration are often experienced. To make life easier, the Dealer Principal decides to keep the franchise Composite in its plastic envelope and places in the bottom drawer of the desk, where it lies in wait, undisturbed and undiscovered.

If the new Dealer Principal survives the next few years, the experience gathered in the job role provides an insight into the financial world and comprehension begins to slowly creep in. Relationships between the numbers, statistics and key performance indicators are realised and the Dealer Principal gains full control of the business. The problem is that the process is very slow and this evolutionary journey of financial discovery for the Dealer Principal has taken many years to gain mastery; it's been long, arduous and unnecessarily difficult. When well-established Dealer

Principals reach the peak of their career, they must all look back and think, *"There must be a better way?"*

Although the story has explained the route beginning from the Sales Department, the journey that commences from Aftersales is just as difficult and torturous: Apprentice to Technician to Foreman to Service Manager and then to Dealer Principal with exactly the same agony along the way.

Viewed from the outside looking in, career progression in a dealership would make a great script for a comedy film if it were not so serious. However, this lack of career development and proper planning has caused another problem which can only be described as "inconsistency".

There are some very good and highly talented Dealer Principals and there are other Dealer Principals that are still evolving who are yet to complete their journey of financial discovery. However, both are teaching their Departmental Managers what they know. This fact dictates that there are some very good and highly talented Department Managers, whilst there are other Department Managers who are being taught by Dealer Principals who do not yet possess mastery of all financial matters.

Sadly, things do not end there because not every Dealer Principal is promoted from being a Department Manager. Now it's time to look at the career path of the person at the other end of the financial spectrum and consider the difficult plight of the Accountant.

Once again there are some very good and highly talented Accountants who really do understand the specifics and uniqueness of the Motor Industry and there are others who are affectionately called "Book Keepers". This is not to say that one is any better than another, it simply illustrates that here we have another opportunity for even more "inconsistency" with the reporting of financial information.

Again we're dealing with generalisations here and there are exceptions to every rule, but a question often asked by departmental Managers is, "Why does the Accountant always make it so difficult for me to understand the accounts?"

Well, contrary to popular belief, the Accountant does not try to confuse a Manager deliberately. When consideration is given to the education process of an Accountant, it's possible to understand why there are so many difficulties with communication between Accountants and Managers, let's take a closer look.

Accountants receive years of training and education to be an Accountant *before* they are promoted into the position. They are fully immersed into a world of double-entry book keeping, auditing, general business principles and taxation. Right from the beginning of their career, they are trained to be an Accountant. It's important to understand that they are not trained to run a dealership or to be a Sales Manager, Service Manager or Dealer Principal. Accountants are trained in international business standards and *general* business applications; *specific* industry knowledge for all Accountants comes much later and only with years of experience within an industry. In reality, it's just as difficult for an Accountant to get a grasp of what is going on at an "operational level" in a dealership as it is for any new Department Manager; again, the evolutionary journey of discovery can take many years to reach fruition.

It's really not surprising that there is a breakdown in communications when Managers converse with Accountants on the subject of Management Accounts because the focus of conversation is centred in different places. For instance, when a Manager asks the Accountant a question about Management Accounts, the Manager is probably asking how this collection of numbers and statistics relate to the operational performance of the department, but the answer that's given by the Accountant is probably focussed on the principles of general accounting practices and how the numbers get to be on each line of the accounts; the two subjects are completely different and hence, more confusion is unwittingly created.

The only solution to this problem is for the Manager and the Accountant to have a high degree of both financial and commercial awareness so that they can share the *right* knowledge and work in synergy with each other. When a team of people talk the same language, share the right knowledge and share a desire for improvement, success is inevitable.

If these two people, who have travelled completely different career paths, converge at a single point in an attempt to communicate, the question must be asked, "What then is the difference between financial awareness and commercial awareness?"

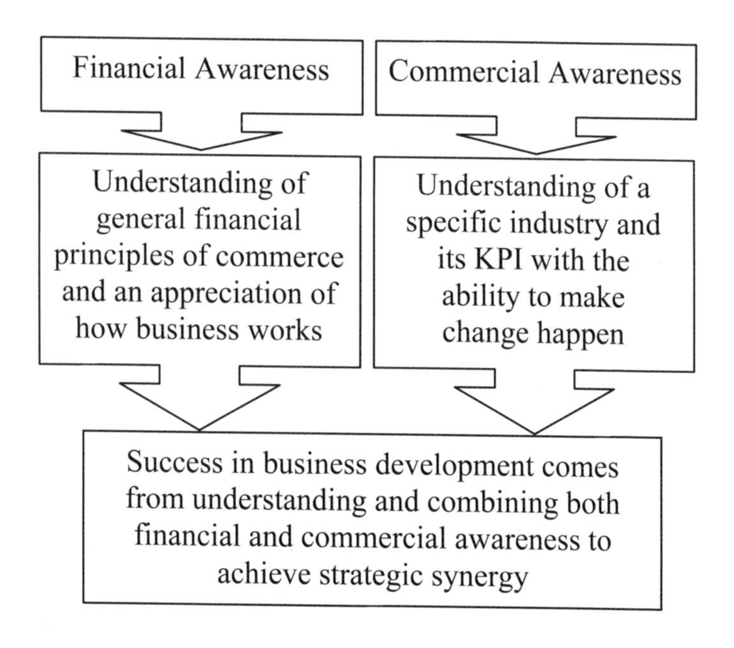

There are Managers in the Motor Industry who have a high degree of commercial awareness. They are the hands-on Managers who get involved with most things and they “know” what’s going on, but they are yet to discover financial awareness. The shortfall here could mean that these Managers are running their business with a blindfold over their eyes because they do not have the ability to track the effects of their actions in the workplace. Running a business blind in this way is very dangerous because more speed in the wrong direction does not help.

On the other hand, there are also Accountants within the Motor Industry who have a high degree of financial awareness. They know the general principles of accounting practices, taxation and they know how to put a set of Management Accounts together, but they are yet to discover commercial awareness and the special intricacies of the Motor Industry. The shortfall here could lead to the Management Accounts being structured for general business practice rather than *specifically* for each department. In other words, they are "mathematically stable" because the bottom line is correct but they are worthless as a management tool.

Unfortunately, this type of *general* accounting may not reflect what is happening at an operational level in each department and therefore KPI output will be inaccurate. Simply having the bottom line of the Management Accounts correct is not enough. In today's trading environment it's absolutely critical for Managers to know *how* they achieve results by measuring their performance trends accurately.

Inaccurate data produces inaccurate analysis.

You can't make a good decision
with bad information.

So now that a few problems have been identified, the question is, "What solutions are required to fix these problems?"

As the opening quotation by Albert Einstein states, *"We cannot solve our problems with the same thinking we used when we created them."* This is indeed profound because it's suggesting that some people need to change the way that they think about things that they currently believe to be true, or in other words, the thinking that got people to understand financial awareness may not be sufficient to get them to understand commercial awareness and vice versa. This is the difficult part because asking someone to change what they believe to be true is often fraught with conflict. This situation brings about a change of paradigm (pronounced paradime).

A change of paradigm is called a *paradigm shift*; think of it as changing from one way of thinking to another. When people fail to make a paradigm shift in business they get left behind and often go bust.

Examples of paradigm shifts are common throughout humanity. In the earliest writings of mankind, it was believed that the Earth was flat and if a ship put to sea and sailed toward the horizon, it would fall off the edge. Later of course, we discovered that the Earth is spherical and this new paradigm changed everything, including the rules of navigation around the planet. Imagine for a moment that a Captain of a ship, out at sea, still believed that the Earth is flat today and he continued to use the old rules of navigation... it would be as effective as trying to find your way around the streets of London with a street map of Paris. Working with the correct paradigm and the correct information is critical for success.

A paradigm shift that changed the world was unveiled in 1543, when on the day of his death, the works of Nicolaus Copernicus were published, which put forward the theory that Earth is not at the centre of the universe with the planets and stars revolving around it. Instead he suggested that the Sun was at the centre of our Solar System and the Earth revolves around the Sun. This was indeed controversial at the time; a huge paradigm shift.

In 1610, sixty seven years after the death of Copernicus, a young scientist named Galileo pointed his new invention, the telescope, at Jupiter and observed the orbits of four of its moons. He believed that there was a force, (which we now know to be gravity) that keeps the moons of Jupiter in their orbits and the same force could keep the Earth's moon in orbit. His observations convinced him that the Earth orbits the Sun along with the other planets. Galileo refuted those who believed that the Sun and all the planets orbited the Earth.

Sadly for Galileo, his new paradigm, or new way of thinking was met with massive resistance and in 1633 he was bought before the Inquisition in Rome and was made to renounce all his beliefs and writings supporting the Copernican theory and he spent the rest of his days imprisoned.

Paradigms Shifts In Business

In his book, *Paradigms*, Joel Arthur Barker wrote a short story about the Swiss watch industry, and now with further research into the subject, the story is expanded here so it's possible to see how paradigm shifts change business, industries and even the world.

Up until 1968, Switzerland had completely dominated the world in the craftsmanship of watch making. Anyone who purchased a watch at that time would be proud to see the words "Swiss Made" embellished on the watch face.

The Swiss were masters of the art and worked ferociously to continually improve their watches to maintain their status in the marketplace. They invented the minute hand, the second hand, smaller dials for 10^{ths} of a second and were at the forefront of waterproofing. Their manufacturing methods for producing minute gears, bearings and main springs were under constant scrutiny and they worked harder and harder to make the very best components in the world. By 1968, it was reported that the Swiss had 65 percent of watch sales world-wide and more than 80 percent of the profits in the market.

The extent of the Swiss domination was colossal and no one was even a close second, yet by 1980, only 12 years later, their market share had collapsed from 65 percent to less than 10 percent. How could such world domination be wiped out in such a short period of time?

The answer is that the Swiss Watchmakers failed to recognise and respond to a new paradigm, the Quartz movement. Their domination in micro-mechanics had given way to the new era of micro-electronics. A new way of measuring time had been developed and everything in which the Swiss had achieved excellence was now totally irrelevant to the new market.

At its peak, the Swiss watch industry employed in excess of 65,000 people to make and construct its mechanical watches and between the years 1979 and 1981, fifty thousand of those people lost their jobs, it was complete devastation for the whole area.

The real tragedy of the story is that it was the Swiss themselves who had invented the Quartz movement at their research and development centre in Neuchâtel, but sadly the Watchmakers rejected the idea because it didn't have any gears, bearings or a main spring. It wasn't a conventional watch of the type they had been making for so many years so it was dismissed without any real thought of the future.

Here's what happened. In 1967, the Swiss Watchmakers allowed the researchers to display their "useless" invention at the World Watch Congress to showcase their skills and innovation in the field of time keeping. The Watchmakers thought it was an interesting gadget, but nothing more than that; it was certainly not considered to be a wrist watch.

The researchers were obviously very proud of their unbelievably accurate time-keeping invention and showed it off to everyone, including representatives of the Japanese giant electronics company, Seiko. After seeing the invention, Seiko immediately went to work on bringing a wrist watch with the Quartz movement to the world-wide market, and as the old saying goes, "the rest is history".

Every year in Neuchâtel, there were prestigious competitions held for the most accurate chronometer, but in 1968, the competitions had to be stopped because of the absolute accuracy of the Quartz movement; it was totally incomparable with conventional mechanical watches. From 1968 onwards, the sales of chronometers plummeted like a falcon diving on its prey and the watches were sold without the prestigious competition certificates.

The Swiss watch industry had collapsed because they failed to see that their industry had changed, they failed to see that the world had changed, they failed to see and accept a new paradigm.

In the early 1980's Nicolas G Hayek, led the recovery from the Swiss watch crisis and in 1983 he formed the Swatch Group of companies.

Swatch adopted the Quartz movement paradigm and the Swiss watch market has recovered its position of being a world leader, but their domination is nowhere near to that of the 1960's.

The Swiss watchmakers only changed their working practices because they were *forced* to change. Their failure to recognise that change is constant and inevitable had cost them supremacy in the global market.

* * * * *

So now you may well be asking the question, how is the Earth being flat, 16th Century theology on the solar system and the Swiss watch-making industry relevant to a book on Management Accounts for the Motor Industry in the 21st Century? The answer is *paradigm shifts*. Whether we look at the 16th Century or the new ideas of today, what is it that prevents us from accepting new ideas? Inaction, inertia, resistance to change, or in other words, failure to recognise and adopt a new paradigm.

People dislike change, yet it is the only thing that brings progress. Comments like, *"But we've always done it this way"* and *"I wasn't taught to do it like that"* are made by people who would have continued with the belief that the Earth is flat. Just like the Swiss Watchmakers of the 1960's, it's possible for business people to be so totally absorbed in what they are doing that their eyes are blind to new methodology.

There have been many new methodologies and paradigm shifts in the Motor Industry that have caused businesses to collapse because they failed to adapt. Some examples are:

Increasing franchise dealer standards
Increasing Overheads
Block exemption
Changes in sales mix between petrol and diesel
Introduction of hybrid vehicles
New vehicle margin reduction
Parallel imports
Just-in-time vehicle ordering
Computing, including DMS
CSI bonus payments and margin hold-back
FSA regulation
Increasing fleet and corporate sales mix
Decreasing return on sales
The Credit Crunch
The collapse of the banking system in 2008
The inability to gain credit
Huge fluctuations in world currencies
Vehicle taxation and government legislation

The list could continue for many pages and the one major paradigm shift that is not included, the one paradigm that is currently having a massive impact and many in the Motor Industry are being left behind, it is of course, the Internet.

For decades, new vehicles have been purchased from dealer showrooms and in recent times, the cost of maintaining these showrooms in line with corporate identity is escalating out of control. Yet, at the same time, the Internet has provided the mechanism for anyone to bypass this traditional showroom route and buy new and used vehicles online from Internet Brokers. New vehicle manufacturers state that 90% of brochure requests are coming from the Internet, new web sites are emerging daily and yet there are still many businesses that do not see the Internet as an immediate priority. These are the businesses that will not be in a position to compete and fend off the Internet Brokers just as the Swiss were unable to compete and fend off Seiko; the Internet is a whole new paradigm for many in the Motor Industry.

Regardless of this fact, Managers running dealerships and Managers running Internet businesses who want to accelerate their business growth both need to communicate well with their Accountants and have a good understanding of their Management Accounts. Working with the right paradigm, the right information and at the right time is critical for success.

Managers and Accountants are working at opposite ends of the same function; one plays the game and the other keeps the score and it's critical that both communicate, understand and speak the same language so that new paradigms can be seen ahead of time and integrated into the core business strategy.

Although this is easy to say, obtaining financial and commercial awareness within the Motor Industry has traditionally been difficult to say the least. It's often cloaked in confusion, secrecy and shrouded in darkness and it's all because of inconsistency which is brought about by Managers and Accountants embarking on long, torturous and evolutionary career paths that fail to converge at a single point and consequently Managers and Accountants are working in the same business, but with different paradigms.

The good news is that whether you are a Manager or an Accountant you'll be delighted to learn that you're no longer subject to this often long and tortuous route. Your journey through this book removes the cloak of confusion and secrecy, cuts through the darkness and illuminates the whole road ahead with absolute clarity. However, let this be a wakeup call. The Motor Industry has witnessed significant change over the last couple of years, it will continue to change over the next couple of years and it will change again in the years after that. It is of critical importance that your Management Accounts reflect these changes if success and in some cases, *survival*, is to be sustained.

The fact that you are holding this book in your hands means that you understand that the way we do business is always subject to change and you readily accept that the structure of Management Accounts that was suitable a decade ago may not be suitable for today's volatile trading environment and changes may be necessary. Although you may be ready for change yourself, for others it might mean a paradigm shift, or in other words, a different way of thinking. Use this book to help you to convey your thoughts and ideas with clarity.

When the phrase, *"But, we've always done it that way"* is heard, jump to attention because that means that old paradigms are still being clutched tightly to the chest and perhaps now is the time to question them.

Accepting that a paradigm shift is necessary takes a great deal of courage, a character trait that few people possess and as a result, the person who suggests that change is necessary, (the paradigm shifter), is often ridiculed as they meet with resistance.

Thankfully, change management today is not as punishing as it was in Galileo's day. However, this book may bring into question and challenge the accounting structure that you currently have in your company, but it is not questioning what you believe to be right or wrong, it's questioning something *much* more important than that... It's questioning whether you are using the correct paradigm and gathering the correct information to survive in the future.

A Call To Action

The world of business is changing at an ever increasing rate and now, the role of the Accountant and the Manager within the Motor Industry has changed significantly because new paradigms are in abundance.

When trading becomes more difficult, the easy route is to reduce head count, marketing and training, but all of these actions may be counter-productive as the resource to grow the business may be removed; it's possible to be efficient, but not effective. Instead, much more focus should be placed on understanding trading difficulties and treating the disease and not the symptoms. This can only be done by ensuring that your business has the best and most useful accounting structure in place to recognise change at the time that it is happening.

Your challenge is to read this book in search of new paradigms, don't fall into the trap of dismissing accounting structures just because they are different. Question *why the differences exist* and how they might serve you better and be more useful than your current accounting structures.

> *"We cannot solve our problems with the same thinking we used when we created them."*
>
> *- Albert Einstein*

PART I

THE PRINCIPLES OF MANAGEMENT ACCOUNTS

CHAPTER I

BREAKING THROUGH THE DEPARTMENTAL JARGON

"If you can't explain it simply, you don't understand it well enough."

- Albert Einstein

CHAPTER I

BREAKING THROUGH THE DEPARTMENTAL JARGON

Due to the diverse nature of a franchised dealership and the different departments evident within, there is so much information that we need to know in order to make the correct strategic decisions and it is because of this that our Management Accounts have evolved to spread over many pages.

On one hand, the amount of information that we receive is an advantage because we can assess all of our strengths and weaknesses. On the other hand, this mass of information can be a daunting to the person who does not understand their full meaning, so let's begin here by breaking down Management Accounts into bite-sized chunks.

The full set of Management Accounts comprises of two separate parts, these being the Profit and Loss Account and the Balance Sheet.

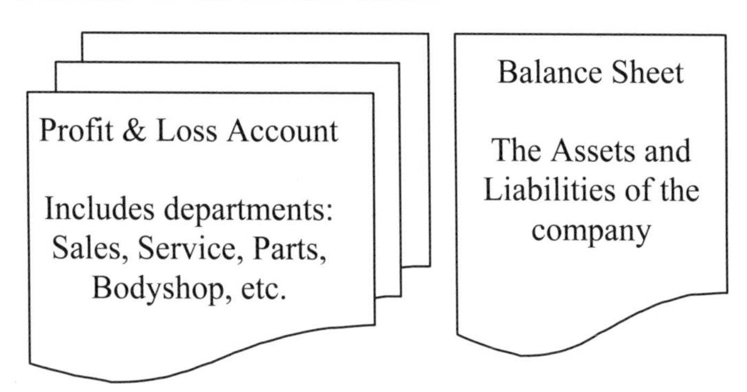

The Profit and Loss Account (P&L) is made up of all of the different departments, which are listed separately and it is this document that most people are referring to when they talk about their Management Accounts.

Many Department Managers only receive a small portion of the Profit and Loss Account which is usually the few pages of accounts for their specific department and they are still referred to as their Management Accounts; albeit a small portion of them.

The Profit and Loss Account contains the income and expenditure in each department or to be more specific, it contains the *invoiced* income and *invoiced* expenditure. It is important to be specific here because the Profit and Loss Account does not state whether or not the goods that have been invoiced have been paid for by the customers.

A company can provide customers with products or services, issue them with invoices which will be shown on the Profit and Loss Account and some customers may pay those invoices whilst other customers may not; the value of the cash outstanding is shown on the Balance Sheet.

There's a world of difference between profit and cash and it's an important principle to understand at this early stage because:

> *A business can survive without any profit,*
> *but it cannot survive without any cash.*

Now the basic difference between profit and cash is in place, let's leave the Balance Sheet behind to revisit it later and move on to discover more about the Profit and Loss Account and the links to operational performance at a departmental level; the bridge between financial and commercial awareness.

The Profit and Loss Account for each department is actually very simple. It doesn't matter how many pages or accounting lines that are present within a department, there are only five basic elements that unlock the power of their meaning. To begin, let's clear up some accounting jargon and take a closer look at these five basic steps.

* * * * *

To get a good grasp of the basics and to avoid any confusion, let's leave the Motor Industry behind for a little while, and return to it later when the basic principles of accounting are in place. Don't overlook the simplicity of this section because it contains the critical building blocks to complete the foundations for understanding all of the departments whether they are contained within a dealership or a stand-alone business; clarity is power. If the right foundations are not in place, it's not possible gain the appropriate understanding.

First, let's take a look at a quick overview of the basic principles of accounting. This is the primary structure for all businesses, regardless of their industry. Once this philosophy is understood, it's easy to get a grasp of everything else that's contained within all departmental accounts.

THE 5 BASIC STEPS OF DEPARTMENTAL ACCOUNTS

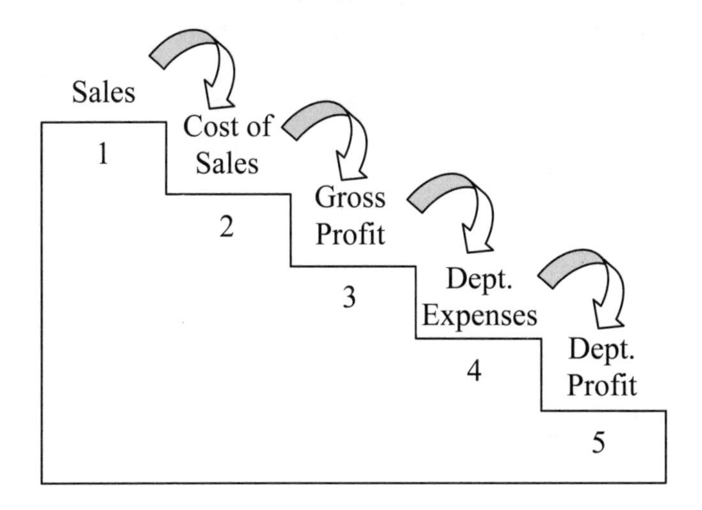

1. Products are sold and an invoice is generated.
2. The cost of the products sold are entered
3. Gross Profit = Sales less Cost of Sales
4. Departmental expenses; some are volume related and some are not.
5. Department Profit = Gross Profit less Expenses.

That's it; it's as simple as that!

It doesn't matter how many pages of accounts are produced for a department, there are still only these five steps to understand. The reason that the Management Accounts cover numerous pages is because there's usually not just one product line that is sold, there are usually at least ten different products and each product has a separate accounting line for sales and cost of sales; that's twenty lines already. Now let's take a closer look at each step in detail.

Step 1: Sales (Turnover)
This is the first line that appears on the departmental Profit and Loss Account and it's expressed as a monetary value representing the invoice value of the products and services that have been sold. This does not mean that these items have been paid for, it simply means that this is the value of the products or services have been sold and invoiced in the reported period.

It represents the value of the products or services that have been sold *after* any discount has been given and it does not include any government taxation such a sales tax or VAT.

Let's say that a product has a retail price of £20 and it's sold for £14, which includes £2 taxation. Here's what happens to the transaction:

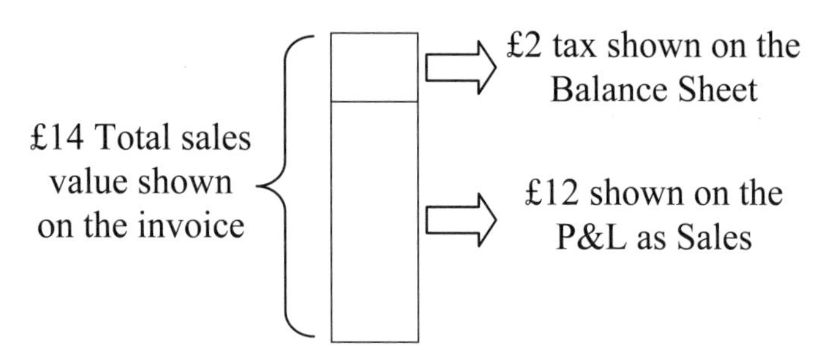

Things to note:

- The retail price (£20) is not usually shown.
- £2 Taxation is not shown on the P&L; it's shown on the Balance Sheet.
- £12 is shown as the Sales or Turnover on the P&L, not the total invoice value of £14.

Sales or Turnover

The monetary value of the products or services that have been sold and invoiced, excluding discount and taxation.

Step 2: Cost of Sales (COS)

Now that a product has been sold and invoiced for £14, the next question is, how much is the purchase price of that product?

There will be invoices from suppliers that confirm that the individual price for each of the products purchased is £8. This is the Cost of Sales and represents only the items sold, it does not include any items left in stock and it does not include any other charges or expenses.

The Cost of Sales does not include expenses such as commission payments, bonuses, cleaning, shipping or postage to the customer, construction, preparation or refurbishment of a product prior to sale or anything else like that. The Cost of Sales refers *only* to the cost of the product or service and anything else is accounted for as a departmental expense. This aspect is *absolutely paramount* to understand for both Managers and Accountants because it is one of the main causes of input error in the Motor Industry.

Cost of Sales

This is the absolute cost of the product or service that has been invoiced. Any other charges are classified as departmental expenses.

Step 3: Gross Profit

This is the first of the profit calculations to be covered and it calculates the difference between the buying price and the selling price of the products that have been invoiced.

It sounds very simple at this early stage, but be warned, many Managers completely overlook the complexity and usefulness of this statistic. Let's begin to put together the Profit and Loss Account for the product sold so far:

Sales	£14
Cost of Sales	£8
Gross Profit	£6

Sales less Cost of Sales = Gross Profit

Now don't get carried away by thinking that this is too simple! Hopefully, it *is* very simple and easy to grasp, but remember that it's only one product at the moment. There are still some very important points to cover here to make sure that interpretation of the whole department with varying sales volumes and multiple product lines is easy to understand.

The secret to the successful analysis of Gross Profit is to be *totally confident* that the Cost of Sales is correct because this can have far-reaching implications and consequences when interpretation of departmental performance is assessed. The Sales or Turnover aspect is relatively straightforward and not often subject to a difference of opinion or interpretation.

The first thing to comprehend is that the term "Gross Profit" is not made up of two random words; they've been put together for a very specific reason.

A dictionary definition of the word "*Gross*" has many variants, but the definition that relates to the meaning of Gross in the context of profit states, "*Without Deduction*".

In a financial context, "*without deduction*" literally means that nothing is taken away, or to be more specific, *no expenses* are taken into account because the difference is between the buying price and the selling price of the products and services that have been invoiced. The next question to ask is, *"Why do we need to measure Gross Profit?"*

To answer this question properly, our sample company is now going expand by buying and selling multiple product lines which sell at different prices and volumes. Firstly, here's the list of inventory:

Category	RRP	Stock	Investment	COS
Product 1	£20	30	£300	£10
Product 2	£12	30	£180	£6
Product 3	£8	30	£90	£3
Product 4	£10	30	£60	£2
Product 5	£15	30	£300	£10
Total	-	150	£930	-

RRP = Recommended Retail Price
Stock = Number of products in stock
Investment = Monetary value of stock
COS = Individual unit cost of each product

Note that the list of inventory has no totals given for the retail prices or the Cost of Sales because they are all different products at different prices; it would be worthless information.

Now let's go into business, generate some sales and show the activity on a Profit and Loss Account.

Example 1:

Sales	£405
Cost of Sales	£217
Gross Profit	£188

Well, it's mathematically stable, but that's all that can be said about it. The problem is that there's not enough information to do any meaningful analysis and it's not possible to see which products have been sold and how well they have performed in terms of sales volume and gross profitability.

Now let's take it to a more "*useful*" level. Briefly study the figures below to see if any insight can be gained into how the products have been selling.

Example 2:

	Unit Sold	Sales	COS	Gross Profit
Product 1	12	180	120	60
Product 2	7	70	42	28
Product 3	5	35	15	20
Product 4	20	120	40	80
Product 5	0	0	0	0
Total	**44**	**405**	**217**	**188**

The information in Example 1 is completely useless for the purposes of analysis. Although it provides the final score, there's no way of knowing *how* it has been achieved. Information such as this is too basic and meaningless because it's not possible to develop a coherent business strategy with such basic information.

The information in Example 2 is much better for analysis, but the problem is that there's six times more information than in Example 1. The important thing to realise here is that although there is more information, it's actually more of the *same* information and *not* completely different information. This is very reassuring because it's still just three lines of accounting; Sales, Cost of sales and Gross Profit.

Now that this additional information is visible, it's possible to see the business activity; what's selling and what's not selling, what's profitable and what's not profitable. When a Manager is armed with this information, would it make a difference to the way they order stocks and run their business in the future? Yes, of course it would. The Manager can now see which products are selling and which ones are not. It's also possible to see which products are being discounted and by how much. This distinction of the different levels of profitability on each different product is critical and it answers the question why there is a need to measure Gross Profit in the first instance. At this stage of trading in any business is very important to understand this simple aspect because it proves a major point in business strategy and analysis:

> *Gross Profit is an **individual product** measure; it is not a departmental profit measure.*

It would be a worthless exercise to calculate an average value for retail prices, invoice prices and Cost of Sales of products and services because strategically, it would not provide any meaningful information. The same is true for Gross Profit because all of the products and services sell in different quantities, they have different sales prices, they have different purchase prices and they have different levels of discount. Analytically speaking, an average Gross Profit for a whole department is completely worthless because the individual product performance is invisible.

Gross Profit is therefore not a departmental measure; it's an *individual product* measure. Information needs to be broken down for each individual product or service that is sold so that it's possible to ascertain how well each individual product or service is being exploited within its marketplace.

The more products and services that a company has on offer, the more information is needed to understand what is happening with each product or service.

There are many different products and service within the Motor Industry and that is the reason why the Profit and Loss Account has evolved to cover so many pages. At first glance it can be daunting, but it's only the same three accounting lines that are separating the many different products and services. To further explain why this is so important, let's take it to extreme. How useful would the Profit and Loss Account be if the Sales, Cost of Sales and Gross Profit were not separated for each department and the results were merged across all departments in a franchised dealership?

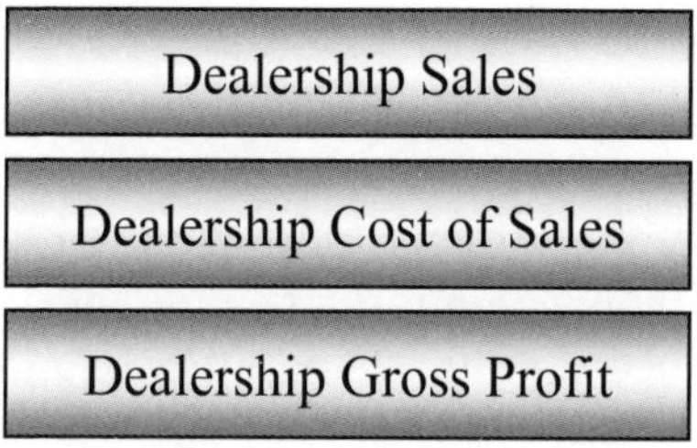

Dealership Sales

Dealership Cost of Sales

Dealership Gross Profit

The result would be analytically useless and deeply frustrating for every Manager involved because it would not be possible to see the contributions from each department; a complete nightmare for everyone.

However, as ridiculous as this may appear, it makes the point very well that averaging and merging data within a department hides what is happening at an operational level. The sales of products and service should be shown separately within a department to illustrate business activity and Gross Profit is not a departmental average; it's an *individual product* measure.

Although this book is not about key performance indicators, Gross Profit is worthy of a little more explanation so that its true power is yielded and not overlooked as is often the case.

Gross Profit, more often than not, is also expressed as a percentage. The formula is Gross Profit ÷ Turnover. (*All profit-related key performance indicators are expressed as a percentage of Turnover).* If a company sells two different products and both of these sell at different sales volumes and profit levels, the Gross Profit percentage figure would be changing every month, based on the sales mix of those products. If those two products were financially merged and reported as a single Gross Profit percentage, it would not be possible to see the different business activities.

To be dynamic and effective, Managers must be able to read the Management Accounts and accurately identify business activity. They must have the ability to separate *Cause* and *Effect*. Cause is the action; Effect is the result of the action.

It's not possible to change an effect. If a different effect (or result) is required, it's the causes that must be changed. Results do not change by themselves, something must act upon them for a change to be realised.

Gross Profit is an Effect. It's the result (or effect) of the Sales and Cost of Sales for each individual product or service within its marketplace.

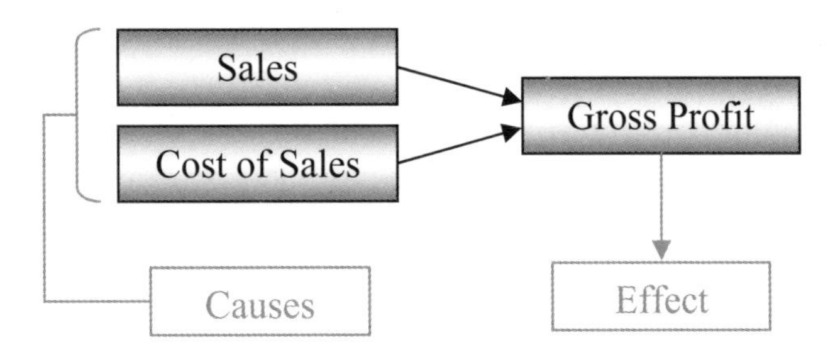

The Sales *causes* may consist of: product availability, product desirability, new model launches, marketing, selling skills, seasonality, pricing and discount strategies etc. The Cost of Sales *causes* may consist of: purchasing skills, bulk buying, product availability, used vehicle appraisal skills etc.

When any of these causes are acted upon and changed, the result (or effect) will be seen in a difference in the reported Gross Profit values and the Gross Profit percentages. The figures for each product and service must be separated and made clearly visible by Accountants so that Managers can correctly identify which causes need to be acted upon for each individual product or service. If data-merge is experienced, Managers lose all the power and are running blind; more speed in the wrong direction does not help. This area will contain more detail within the departmental sections to ensure that Accountants and Managers work together, with the same paradigm.

Step 4: Expenses

Departmental expenses often cause a lot of confusion in conversations between Managers because different terminology is used by different people and different organisations. However, although the terminology is different, the basic rules are exactly the same, which thankfully means that all of this confusion can be completely eradicated.

The first thing to understand is that there are two different kinds of expenses within a department and they work in completely different ways. The differences between the two expenses and the way that they work is very easy to explain, the only confusing part is that the words used to describe them are sometimes different for the franchises, dealers and independent businesses. Having made this statement, it's not nearly as complicated as it sounds because the underlying principles are exactly the same.

This section explains the differences between the functionality of departmental expenses and what causes them to rise and fall. In addition to that, it will also eliminate the confusion around the various terminology used by different people, which is illustrated by showing two different options.

Firstly, let's begin with Option 1 and the words and expense terminologies that most manufacturers and franchises use in their composites and financial reports:

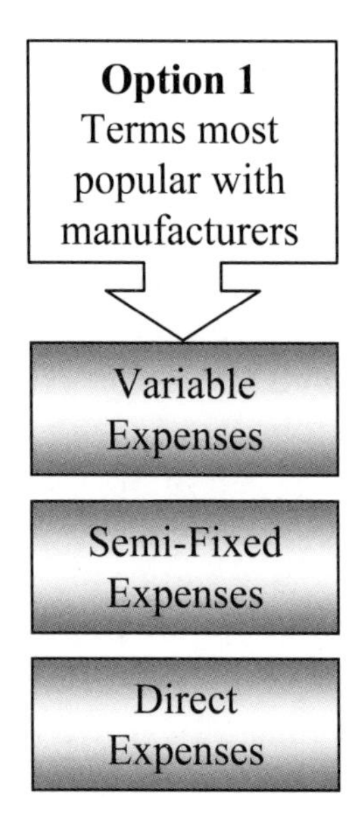

Variable Expenses

The term, "Variable" might suggest that this is an expense that *changes or varies* each month. Well, that is correct, but the question is, what is it exactly about this expense that changes or varies?

The *logical* way to think here would be that this is an expense where the *value* changes or varies each month. In other words, if an expense is £1,000 for one month and in the next month it is £2,000 then the *value* of the expense has varied therefore it is a variable expense. Well, this is a *logical* conclusion, but it is incorrect.

The golden rule for understanding the terminology surrounding departmental expenses is that the terminology is not related to *values* at all, but rather to *sales volumes*.

The term "Variable" in the context of expenses does not mean that these are expenses that have varying *values*. Variable in this instance means that these are expenses that change or vary with sales *volume*. In other words, when a company sells more products, the variable expenses increase. The opposite is also true; when fewer products are sold, variable expenses decrease.

A good example of a Variable Expense would be Sales Commission. Every time a product or service is sold, the sales team receive a commission payment. The more products that are sold, more commission payments are made. The fewer products sold, fewer commission payments are made. Commission is classified as a Variable Expense because it *varies* with the sales volume of products or services that are sold. In summary then, Variable Expenses are departmental expenses that are triggered by selling something; in other words, they are a *consequence* of sales volume.

Semi-Fixed Expenses

Now that the meaning of "Variable", is in place, understanding the term "Semi-Fixed" is going to be very simple because it's the exact opposite.

The term "Semi-Fixed" means that there are expenses within the department that will be evident whether any products are sold or not. These expenses are not related to the volume of sales and they are all under the control of Management.

As stated earlier, there are two different types of expenses within a department and they work in different ways. Therefore if Variable can be defined as "*Departmental expenses that are triggered by sales volume*", then Semi-Fixed can be defined as, "*Departmental expenses that are **NOT** triggered by sales volume*".

A good example of a Semi-Fixed expense would be advertising. A company might spend £1,000 on advertising its products and additional products may be sold as a direct result of the advertisement or on the other hand, no additional products might be sold.

The point here is that it is the Manager who decides when to advertise and how much to spend and the expense is still evident whether any more products are sold or not.

A further example of both types of expenses would be the total salary of the Salespeople because this is shown in two different places. The commission payments would be shown as a Variable expense and will rise and fall with the sales volume and the basic wage would be shown as a Semi-Fixed expense because that remains static and is not affected by sales volume. Both of the elements that make up the total salary of a Salesperson (basic wage plus commission) are controlled in different ways and therefore they are reported within different categories.

Critical Point of Understanding

Within a department, there are two different categories of expense. One category is triggered by sales volume, (Variable) whilst the other category is not triggered by sales volume, (Semi-Fixed).

This is very important to understand because the actions required to take control of Variable Expenses are very different actions that are required to take control of Semi-Fixed Expenses

THE DANGER ZONE

Some Profit and Loss Accounts do not make the distinction between the two categories of expenses and the all departmental expenses get thrown together in one pot. *Beware*; this accounting format can be very dangerous because Managers will not be able to accurately identify and isolate any problem areas that exist. Consider this scenario:

Imagine that a Manager is confronted by the boss with this statement: *"I've looked at the accounts for this month and the Departmental Expenses are too high, you need to get them down and you need to do it quickly. Come and talk to me this time next week about the changes you are making".*

The question that follows in the mind of the Manager can only be, *"What actions do I need to take in order to bring the departmental expenses down?"*

Before doing anything, the Manager first needs to know *which category* of expense is too high. They must understand that some expenses are triggered by sales volume and other expenses remain in place whether sales volume increases or not. Obviously, the actions required to keep them under control are different for each type of expense, so what is the Manager to do?

If the departmental expenses are not separated into the separate categories, how does the Manager know what actions to take?

Perhaps more importantly, if departmental expenses are not categorised correctly, how will the Manager measure the effects of the actions taken upon operational performance and how will they know if they're doing the right thing?

When the difference between Variable and Semi-Fixed is not understood or separated on the accounts, this lack of knowledge has the potential to wreak havoc. In one instance, the Manager could work at reducing the Semi-Fixed expenses (without knowing that of course) at a time when sales volume is increasing. The result could be very frustrating if not understood because in this instance, the departmental expenses could be increasing because the sales volume is increasing. Variable expenses could be rising at a greater rate than the Manager is able to decrease the Semi-Fixed expenses and the departmental expenses end up higher than before any changes were made.

The Manager's comprehension of how these two different expenses are triggered and controlled and the correct coding of the Nominal Ledger by Accountants is paramount to the success of all businesses. It's not possible to make a good decision with bad information. Correct separation of these two categories is crucial to making the right operational decisions.

Direct Expenses

Where the terms Variable and Semi-Fixed are evident, the term "Direct Expenses" is simply the sum total of both. In other words, this relates to the total expenses for the whole department and might sometimes be called "Departmental Expenses".

As the previous scenario suggests, by itself, it's analytically worthless without the proper split between the two expense categories because Managers and Accountants need *visibility* of the activities that generated those expenses.

Whilst it may be useful to view the total department expenses as a total, understanding how the total has been arrived at is far more useful and important because it's an effect, not a cause.

Now that the different categories of departmental expenses in Option 1 are understood together with the principles under which they work, let's take a look at Option 2, the alternative terminology that is most common in accounts of franchised dealers, independent Service Centres, Parts Factors and Bodyshops.

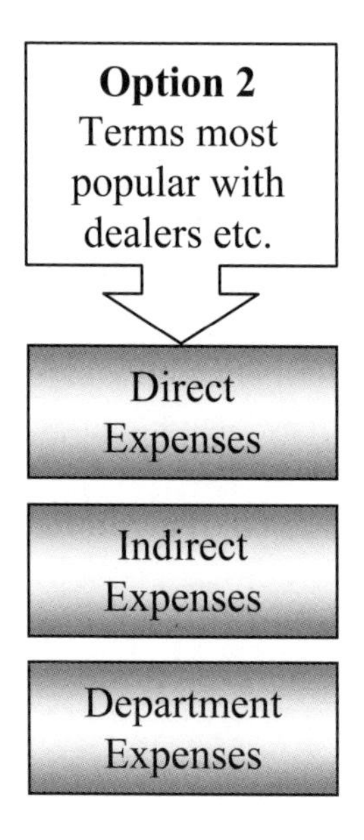

OK, so the wording has changed, but that's all that's changed, nothing else has changed and the basic principles of accounting are the same.

The layout of Option 2 is the same as Option 1, therefore in Option 2, "Direct" has the same meaning as "Variable" and "Indirect" has the same meaning as "Semi-Fixed".

In this layout, Direct Expenses are departmental expenses that are triggered by Sales Volume and Indirect Expenses are departmental expenses that are not triggered by sales volume. The words have changed but the rules governing how the expenses controlled and shown on Management Accounts have not changed.

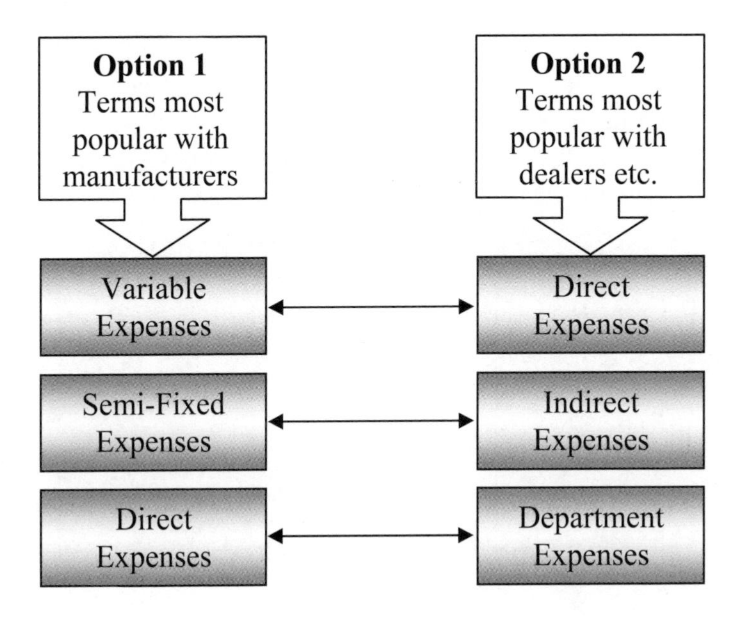

Now let's deal with some confusion that might exist. The term "Direct Expenses" as seen in Option 2 above, is also used in Option 1, but it's positioned in a different place and it's used to describe a different category of expense.

Now that this potential confusion has been uncovered, it's important to keep it in mind when communicating with other people on the subject because the words

"Direct Expenses" can have two completely different meanings. If left unquestioned, this could lead to inconsistencies in discussions about performance development. When involved in a meeting someone might make a comment such as, *"My Direct Expenses are increasing, are you experiencing the same problems?"* But what are they really asking?

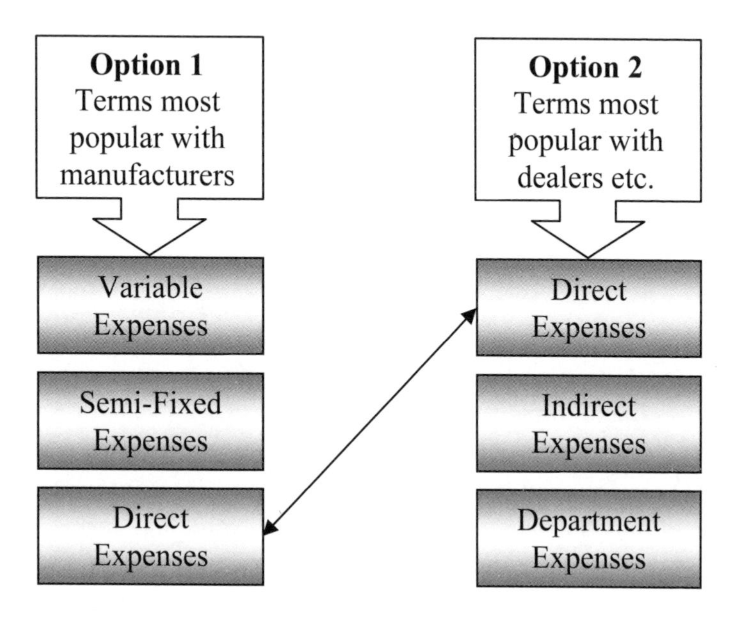

This question needs clarification because the term "Direct Expenses" has two different meanings and a failure to seek clarification on this matter could result in unnecessary conflict.

To avoid this possible divergence, the simple question to be asked is something like this: *"Direct Expenses. Do you mean my total departmental expenses or do you mean only those departmental expenses that are triggered by sales volume?"*

One of two things will happen now. The other person will either confirm exactly what they mean or they will look at you like you're from another planet. If the other person looks confused by the question, you'll know exactly what the problem is; they don't understand that there are two different categories of expenses within a department and therefore they don't understand this conflict in terminology. If you find yourself in this situation, there's really no point continuing with the conversation unless you decide to educate them on the differences between the two. *Perhaps you could recommend a good book ☺.*

The cross-use of the term "Direct Expenses" happens very frequently, especially with Managers and Accountants inside different businesses so be aware of the question and the possible inconsistency that may lie ahead.

The terms contained within Option 1 are more commonly used by manufacturers and franchises on their composite and financial reports and the terms used in Option 2 are more commonly used by dealers and independents. Neither of them is right nor wrong; they are different words that are used to name the same category of expenses.

This difference in terminology may appear confusing at first, but the fact that there is different terminology used to explain the same things should not be of any concern. The only thing that's important is that there is sufficient clarity to understand the logic behind the terminology and relate it to the basic principles of accounting. When this level of clarity is established, the power lies in the hands of the Manager because they have the knowledge and the ability to take the appropriate actions at the right time to improve performance when it is necessary rather than being bemused and bewildered by other people's terminology and poor clarity.

Step 5: Department Profit

With all confusion and cross-terminology used to describe expenses out of the way, understanding Departmental Profit is a breeze. It's what's commonly called "the bottom line". This is simply the profit that's left in the department after all expenses have been deducted. The mathematical formula is:

Gross Profit – Dept. Expenses = Department Profit

There may be a little confusion surrounding this part of the Profit and Loss Account because it's only one of the many different names by which this is known. Other words and terminology include:

- Department Profit
- Direct Profit
- Operating Profit
- Direct Operating Profit
- Departmental Operating Profit
- Contribution
- Departmental Contribution
- Operating Contribution
- Direct Contribution

No matter which term is used, the formula for its calculation is always the same.

The one term that may cause a little confusion is Net Profit because the word "Net" denotes a total business profit rather than a departmental profit. Therefore it is extremely rare that the term Net Profit is shown within a department.

The dictionary definition of the word, "Net or Nett", in a financial context is: "*Remaining after all deductions*".

At a departmental level, "*all deductions*" have not yet been accounted for, only those deductions within a department. Company Overheads are still to be deducted to get down to the "Net" Profit level.

The term "Net or Nett" is reserved to describe the whole business operation or the whole dealership result rather than an individual departmental result. However, just because the term Net Profit should not be seen within a department doesn't necessarily mean that people won't use the term Net Profit when talking about department profit! Be aware of this fact and establish clarity in all communications by asking a question such as, *"Do you mean the bottom line profit of the department, or the bottom line profit of the whole business?"* Once the answer is obtained there will be no doubt about the issues surrounding the rest of the conversation. Clarity is power.

In summary then, understanding the Profit and Loss Accounts is really quite easy and straightforward. Once it is realised that there are only five basic steps, it takes away any confusion that may exist.

When the departmental Profit and Loss Account is expanded over many pages, it doesn't mean that it appears to be more complicated because there are still only five basic steps to consider.

In reality, the more pages that are produced on the Profit and Loss Account the better it is because that means that there is more detailed information on *each* of the five steps and that puts the dialogue between Managers and Accountants in a much stronger position; it's easier to understand and explain. The more detailed the information, the better the analysis can be and that can only lead to greater business development and higher profitability.

"If you can't explain it simply,
you don't understand it well enough."

- Albert Einstein

OVERVIEW OF THE FIVE BASIC STEPS

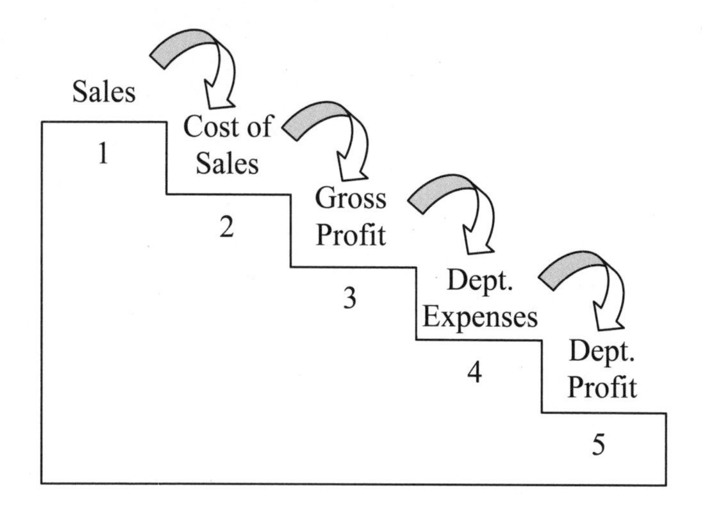

1. Products are sold and an invoice is generated.
2. The cost of the products sold are entered
3. Gross Profit = Sales - Cost of Sales
4. Departmental expenses; some are volume related and some are not.
5. Department Profit = Gross Profit - Expenses.

That's it; it's as simple as that!

Keep this simple model in mind to cut through the financial fog, haze and confusion that exists with the diverse terminology that different people use to explain the same thing. At the end of the day, no matter how complex the Profit and Loss account might first appear to be, there are after all, only five basic steps.

Option 1: Overview of Department Structure
(Terminology mostly used by the manufacturer)

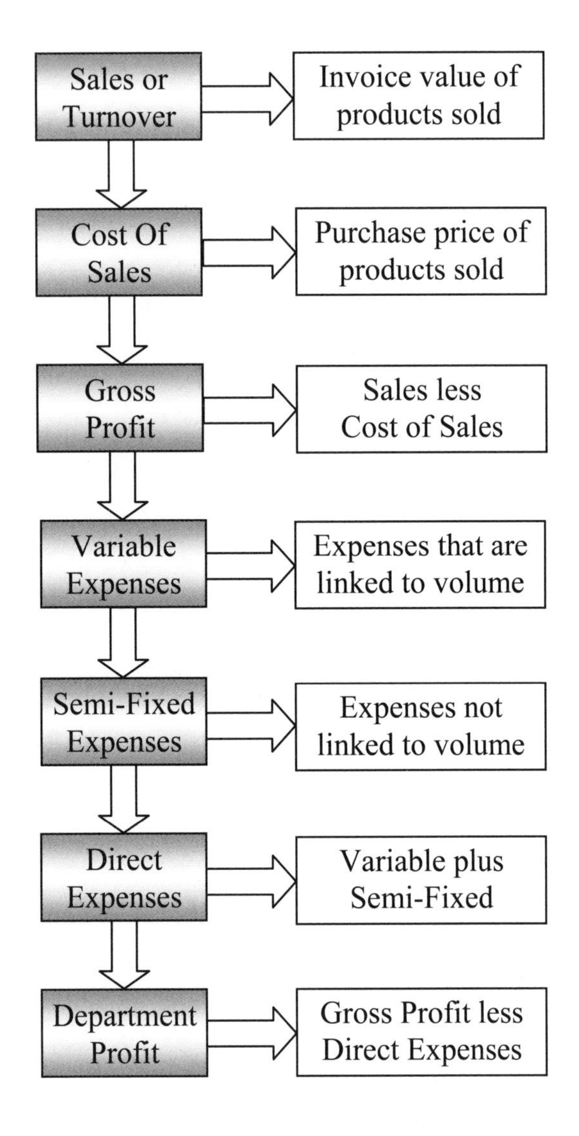

Option 2: Overview of Department Structure

(Terminology mostly used by dealers)

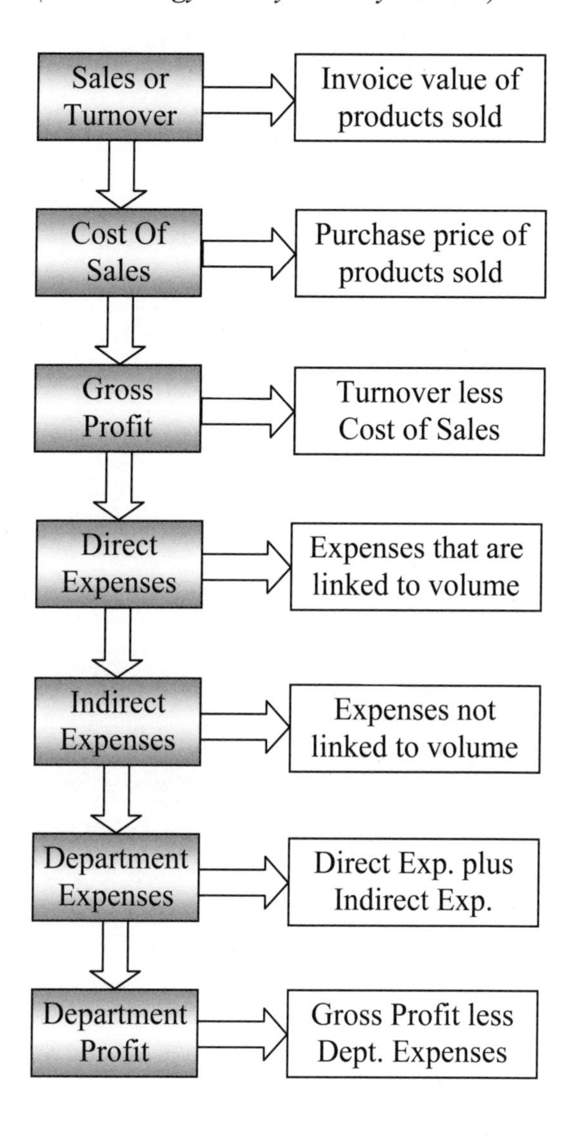

CHAPTER II

UNDERSTANDING OVERHEADS

"Businesses planned for service are apt to succeed; businesses planned for profit are apt to fail."

- Nicholas Murray Butler

CHAPTER II

UNDERSTANDING OVERHEADS

Overheads are recorded separately to the department statistics because these areas are about the business as a whole rather than the operational aspect of the department. They're usually left for the attention of the General Manager and Accountant rather than the Department Manager because there's very little that a Departmental Manager can influence.

Overheads
These are general business expenses that are outside of the department, they are not linked with sales volume or operational activities. Examples of some Overheads might be:

Rent
Rates
Lighting, heating and power
Head Office Charges
General Management Salaries
Audit and Legal Fees
Computer Costs
Printing and Stationery
Interest charges
Building Maintenance
Insurance
Security
Vehicle Running Costs

Overheads is one term that is used to describe these expenses and there are a few other terms that mean the same thing such as, Fixed Expenses or Indirect Expenses. Here's where a little confusion might begin to creep in again because the term "Indirect Expenses" is sometimes used within a department to categorise those expenses that are not related to sales volume. Now let's revisit the two options in expense terminology from Chapter I and add the general business expenses to the list to clear up this possible confusion.

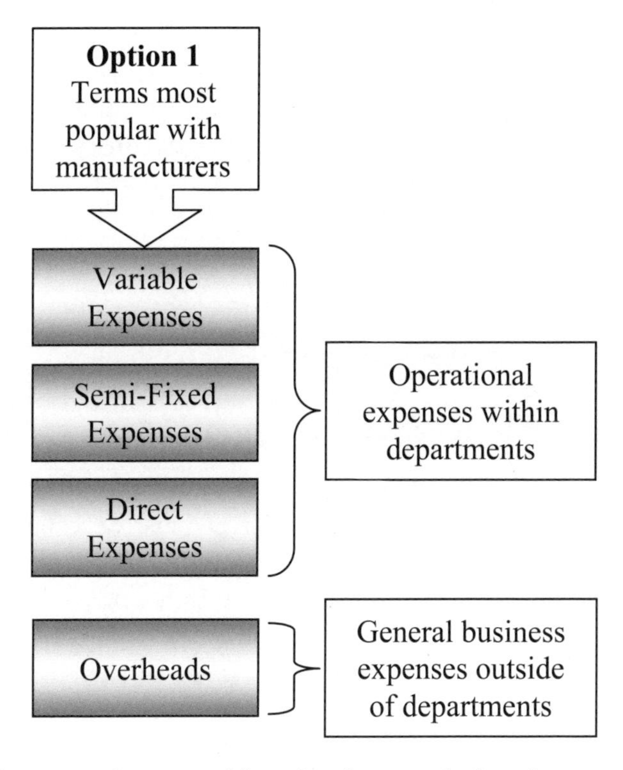

In this example everything is clear and there's no cross-use of terminology that may give rise to confusion. Now let's look at Option 2.

In this example there is cross-use of the term Indirect Expenses, which is used to categorise non-volume related departmental expenses and general business expenses.

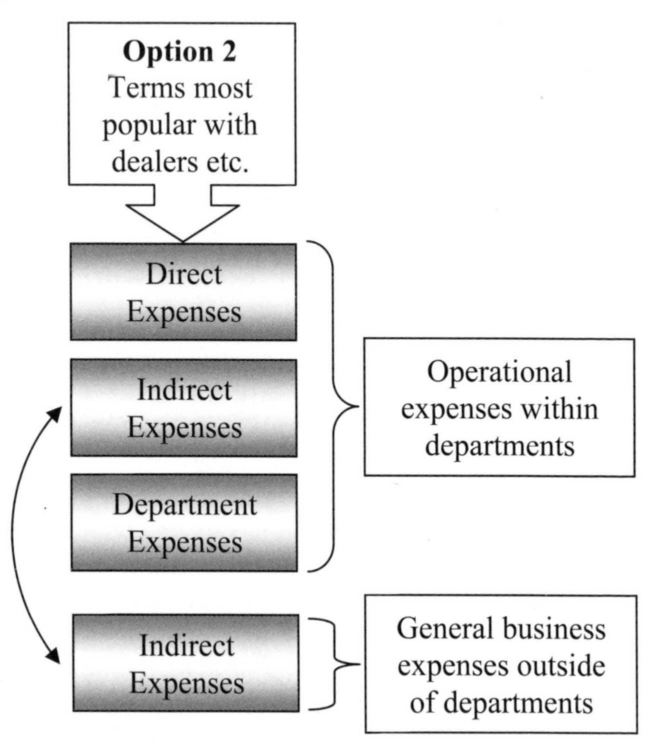

Here's a situation where clarity must be established with other people so that meaningful communications can take please when discussing Indirect Expenses.

In discussions with people from other businesses, someone might make a comment such as, *"My Indirects are too high, they're continuing to rise and they killing profitability. Is anyone else having the same problems?"* The problem here is that it is not totally clear what the question is asking and clarity must be established before the conversation can continue with any real meaning. To establish clarity, a question such as this must be asked:

"You say that your Indirects are too high. Indirect Expenses have two meanings, so let's understand which one we're talking about here so that we can help each other. In your particular case, are you referring to the departmental expenses that are not triggered by sales volume, or are you referring to the general business overheads that are shown on the back page that are outside of the departments?"

If this distinction is not established, confusion could win the day and the meeting could end in conflict. Clarity is power.

When faced with these problems of the cross-use of terminology, almost everyone asks the question, "Why do we have so many different terms in the Motor Industry that mean the same thing making Management Accounts so unnecessarily complicated and confusing?" Well, if the Motor Industry were to unify its terminology in all financial matters, everything would be much easier to understand and there would be far less confusion. However, it's most unlikely that this will ever happen because there are different manufacturers from different countries and different Accountants from different industries, all of whom have their own versions and methodology. However, wouldn't it be nice if we all followed a single path?

While unification of terminology is a nice dream to hold on to, the reality of the situation for today is that clarity must be sought to move business forward and in truth, it's really not that difficult, it simply requires an in depth knowledge of the subject and a few questions aimed in the right direction. Although terminology may be different, the basic principles of accounting are the same.

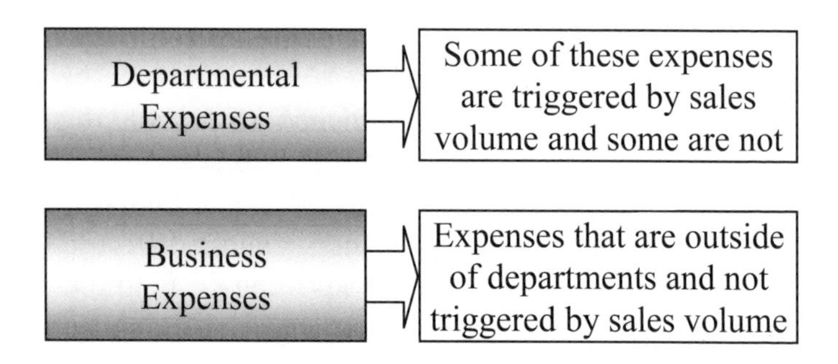

Once these different categories of expenses are understood and what kinds of actions affect them, the fact that different terminology is used to describe them is a small matter of little significance. Clarity is power.

Now that the cross-use of terminology for describing expenses is cleared up, let's take a look at an accounting anomaly that exists with general business overheads.

There are very rare occasions, or to be more specific, there are very few businesses today who continue with a practice known as "apportionment". This practice is where the Accountant apportions or shares some of the Overheads across the departments. For instance, the Rent may be apportioned or shared between Sales, Service Parts and Bodyshop and not shown in the Overheads at all.

Applying apportionment to Overheads is exceedingly rare nowadays because it is widely recognised that it distorts the interpretation of operational performance within the departments, especially when comparing operational performance with different businesses.

Apportionment can also lower the morale and motivation of the Department Manager because the Overheads that are added or apportioned to the department are outside of the Manager's control. This practice makes operational results look worse than they really are and when compared to other businesses that do not practice apportionment there are large variances in the results. When this happens, it is not uncommon to see a Departmental Manager who has been subject to the practice of apportionment to "give up" on any meaningful analysis and the business suffers as a result.

Managers within the Motor Industry thrive on comparing information with each other to glean Best Practice strategies and ideas, but if the input data has inconsistencies like some Accountants engaging in apportionment whilst other Accountants do not, then it becomes very difficult to identify comparative strengths and weaknesses between different businesses. It's not possible to make a good decision with bad information. It is for these reasons that the practice of apportionment is considered bad accounting practice.

One of the main problems with the Overheads of a franchised dealership that they have been growing exponentially over the last decade due to higher locations costs, franchise dealer standards and ever-increasing Head Office Charges.

As these three factors continue to increase, the dealership becomes more dependent on borrowed funds and as a direct result, Interest Charges continue to increase. The relentless pressure from all of these expenses reduces Net Profit like a gale-force wind and torrential rain erodes a cliff-face.

It's a constant battle balancing the cost of the business overheads, profitability and customer satisfaction. To achieve success, Accountants and Managers must work together in synergy, but they often work at opposite ends of the spectrum.

Generally speaking, the Accountant focuses on reducing expenses in any way possible, but if the balance is upset and too much expense is stripped away, the danger is that too many resources are removed and the business loses the ability to exploit the marketplace and look after customers correctly. On the other hand, Managers generally increase resources in an attempt to infiltrate the marketplace and grow the business, but if this balance is upset and expenses are too high, any profitability gains will be instantly eradicated.

Controlling Overheads is a delicate balance and one that ought to be tempered with good reason, sound common sense and a business strategy that includes the right knowledge and synergy between financial and commercial awareness. In other words, Managers and Accountants need to understand each other, work together and move the business in the same direction at the same time. Relationships of this kind do not happen by luck or by chance, they evolve by all parties being interested in developing themselves and seeking to help others. Resources should not be stripped away simply to save money, not should they be added with reckless abandon. Overheads need to be carefully balanced so that the right levels of customer care is achievable.

"Businesses planned for service are apt to succeed; businesses planned for profit are apt to fail."

- Nicholas Murray Butler

CHAPTER III

UNDERSTANDING NET PROFIT

"I've made the tough decisions,
always with an eye toward the bottom line."

- Donald Trump

CHAPTER III

UNDERSTANDING NET PROFIT

"The bottom line" is a phrase well used by many people in business and it's not just limited to profit. This colloquialism usually means, "What is the end result?" When conversations fail to get to the point quickly enough, someone might be heard to say, *"Stop waffling and just get to the point; what's the bottom line?"*

When the phrase "The bottom line" is used in a financial context, the logical assumption is for it to be referring to the last line of the Profit and Loss Account. Well, in some cases that may be correct, but then again, it may not. For instance, if the term is used by a Departmental Manager, "The bottom line" might well be referring to the bottom line of the department. However, if the term is being used by a General Manager or an Accountant, "The bottom line" might be referring to the bottom line of the business as a whole, not just a department. Once again, questions must be asked in order to establish clarity on the subject.

"*The bottom line*" is not the only colloquialism in use, other terms include "The bottom right-hand corner" because this is where the profit figures are located on the Profit and Loss Account. It's easy to understand why these terms exist, but there is a world of difference between the bottom line of a department and the bottom line of the whole business and the term that distinguishes the difference between the two profit measurements is the term "Net". A dictionary definition of the term "Net" (or Nett, they mean exactly the same thing), is given as, *"Remaining after all deductions"*.

In a financial context, when the term profit is preceded by the word Net as in "Net Profit", this means that this is the profit that remains after all expenses for the whole business have been deducted. To be more specific, the term Net Profit should not be used within a department because it is a term that's reserved for referring to the business as a whole. It's the profit in the company that is *remaining after all deductions*.

The easy way to think about Net Profit is to take the profit made by each of the departments, deduct the Overheads of the business and Net Profit is what is remaining.

However, just to confuse things a little, there is not just one definition of Net Profit, there are two different types: Net Profit Before Interest and Net Profit Before Tax.

Let's take a look at the overall view of the Profit and Loss Account in a schematic form of a franchised dealership and then the differences between these terminologies, Net Profit will be much easier to understand. Although this model is illustrating a franchised dealership, the same principles are true for the independent business, the only difference being that that there may only be a single department as opposed to five departments.

Overview of a dealership Profit and Loss Account

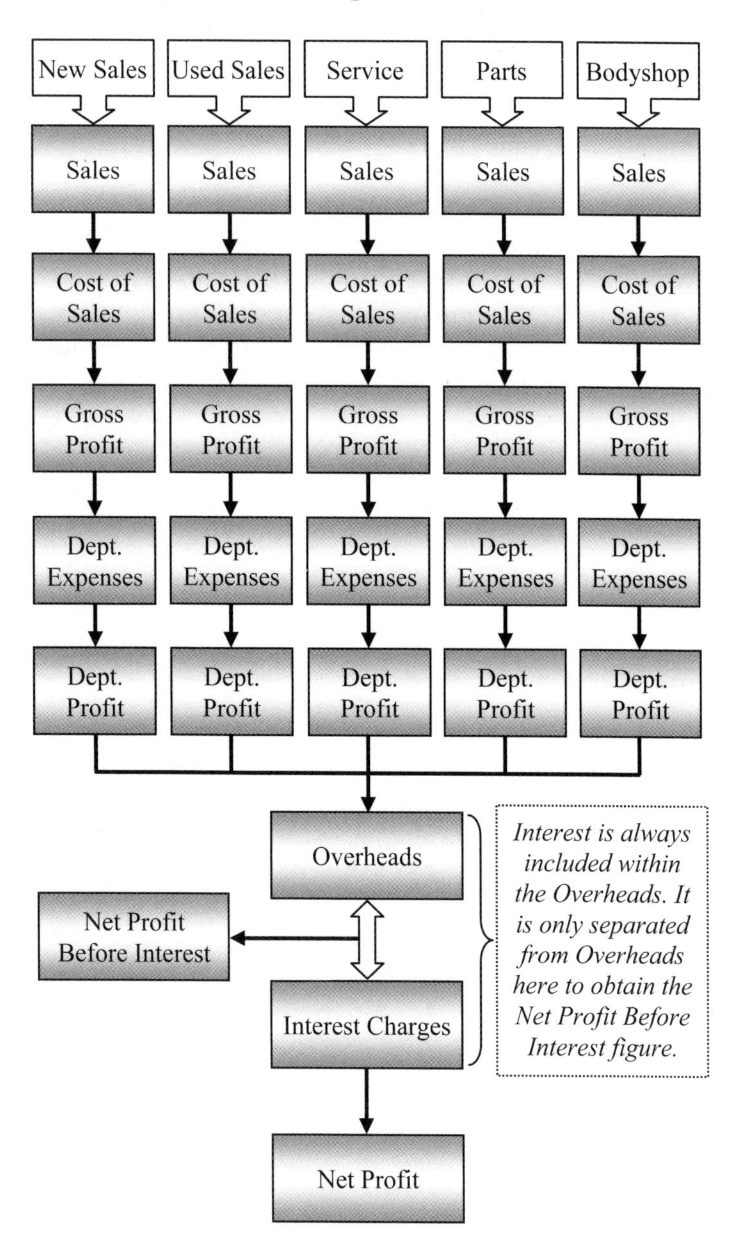

Net Profit Before Interest (NPBI)
This may sometimes be called EBIT, which means Earnings Before Interest and Tax. As the Profit and Loss overview illustrates, this is the collection of the Department Profits, less all of the business Overheads with the exception of Interest Charges.

Interest Charges are excluded from this profitability measure because Interest is a direct result of how much money a company borrows. When Interest Charges are removed, it's possible to compare different businesses without the distortion of how they are funded.

Example:

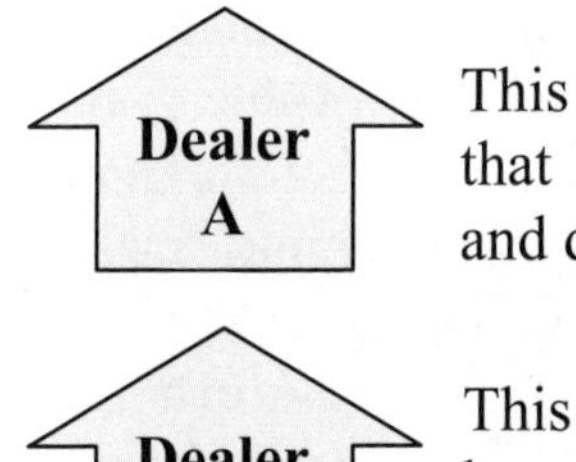

This is a well established business that has been in situ for 35 years and does not have any loans.

This is a new business that has been in place for 2 years; it has loans of £1.8 million.

In this extreme example, Dealer B would have very high Interest Charges and Dealer A would not have any Interest Charges at all. To be able to compare these two companies more realistically, the Interest Charges are excluded purely to calculate Net Profit Before Interest so that the operational side of the businesses can be compared. How the two different companies are funded and how much Interest is payable is a completely different matter altogether.

When capital investment in modern-day dealerships is considered, it's highly unlikely that any two businesses have exactly the same level of borrowings and have been funded in exactly the same way with exactly the same interest charges from the bank. Therefore it's safe to assume that no two businesses pay the same amount in Interest Charges, which means that when comparing overall operational performance, Interest Charges should be removed from the Overheads to create Net Profit Before Interest so that a level playing field between businesses is created. Note that Interest Charges still remain within the business Overheads, they are only excluded from the Overheads purely for the calculation of Net Profit Before Interest.

When comparing performance with other businesses, Net Profit Before Interest as a monetary value is not much use because all businesses have different levels of sales, therefore it must be converted into a Key Performance Indicator, which is achieved by expressing it as a percentage of Turnover. NPBI% is the last of the "Operational" profitability measures and it's useful for assessing a franchise proposition in the marketplace. In other words, this key performance indicator can be used to compare individual business performance, but it can also be used to compare the strength of one franchise dealer network with another franchise dealer network to assess the viability of each franchise without the distortion of funding.

Net Profit

This is "the bottom line" of the business as a whole. Its basic formula is total sales, less all of the cost of sales and all expenses, departmental and Overheads including Interest charges. This is the Net Profit Before Interest calculation, but now with the Interest Charges being taken into account. This is expressed as a percentage of Sales and usually called Return on Sales (ROS). It's useful to track and trend your own business growth, but it's not as useful as NPBI% for comparing one business with another because Return on Sales contains the distortion of Interest Charges, which is different for everyone.

The Danger Zone

There are many non-franchised sales outlets, independent workshops and Bodyshops that do not separate operational expenses from business Overheads. Statistics become merged, analysis is compressed and the basic Profit and Loss Account structure looks something like this:

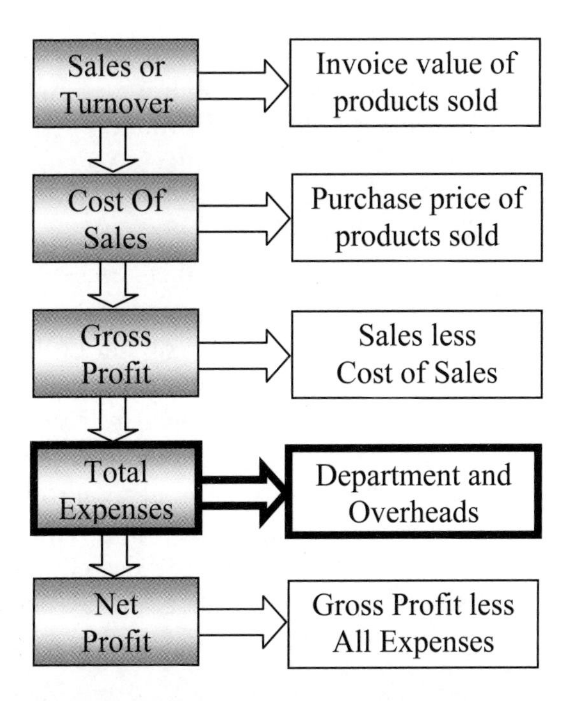

When the Profit and Loss Account is simplified to this basic level is becomes dangerous because it's much more difficult to see how business can be improved. Whilst the bottom line or the Net Profit will be the same whether data separation is evident or not, the main point of the Profit And Loss Account is missing because it not possible to see *how* the Net Profit has been generated.

Results are important, but not nearly as important as knowing how you've achieved them.

If the business produced a poor Net Profit last month, how can it be improved next month? If the business produced a good Net Profit last month, how can it be repeated next month?

The bridge of knowledge that spans the gap between financial and commercial awareness is forged on the anvil of clarity. If Managers cannot use the Profit and Loss Account to identify the results of their actions at an operational level, the Management Accounts are rendered worthless as a management tool. Clear separation and identification of operational activity is critical if Managers are to use their Management Accounts to understand their business performance. The methodology for the structure of the Profit and Loss Account for a franchised dealership with departmental expenses being separated from business overheads as explained earlier should not be any different whatsoever to the structure of the Profit and Loss Account for an independent, non-franchised business; they are both the same in the context of reporting business activity. Making things simpler and compressed is a disadvantage to business growth.

Busting An Urban Myth

When the Net Profit is transferred from being a monetary value into a percentage of Turnover, it's know as Net Profit%, or more commonly it's known as Return on Sales. Some people are often heard saying that Return on Sales in the Motor Industry is too low at 2% and they put forward the argument that, *"My money would be better invested in a Bank"*. This argument is totally wrong and shows a lack of real understanding for Return on Sales; it's not the same as Return on Investment, which is what you get from the Bank.

Example:

a) Sales	= £10,000,000
b) Investment	= £952,380
c) Net Profit	= £200,000
d) Return on Sales	= 2% (c ÷ a x 100)
e) Return on Investment	= 21% (c ÷ b x 100)

In the example above, the Return on Sales is a lowly 2%, but that is the Net Profit % on the Sales. The Net Profit % on the investment, or the Return on Investment (ROI) is reported at 21%, a far higher return than is possible to obtain from investing the money in a Bank.

The value of investment in a business is *not* equal to the value of Sales. In other words, if a business has Sales of £10 million, it does not require £10 million investment because the investment is re-used; money comes in and goes out multiple times as the company buys and sells its products.

When the argument of, *"My money would be better invested in a Bank"* is raised in future discussions, it should be related to the Return on Investment as opposed to Return on Sales because the Investment in a company would be the amount that would be invested in a Bank, not the Sales.

The Return on Investment for a franchised dealership is around 21%, which is considerably better than the putting it into a Bank which usually sits around 6% of the investment.

Effects Of Diminishing Profit

There's always a lot of discussion surrounding Return On Sales at business meetings and the discussion is usually focussed on it reduction, but as strange as it may seem, falling Net Profit is not really something to be overly concerned about.

Firstly, it's important to understand that these discussions are based on Return on Sales expressed as a percentage rather than a monetary value and it's the trend of this key performance indicator that has been diminishing over previous years.

The fact that this key performance indicator is falling is not good news, but many Managers are focussing their attentions in the wrong area because Return on Sales % will continue to fall over the forthcoming years and here's the reasons why...

Let's take a closer look at the Department Profit% so that the big picture can be seen in more detail. The figures in the diagram are for illustration purposes only; the important factor here is the difference between the profit margins shown in each department.

Relationship of Department Profit And Net Profit

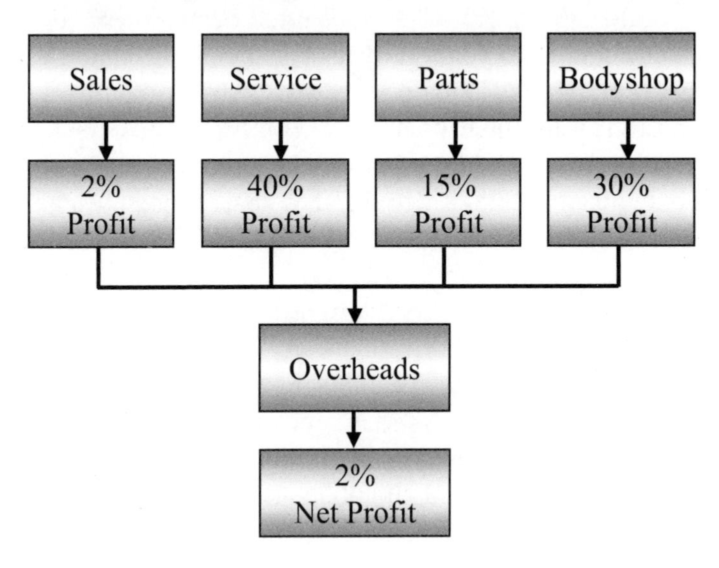

This illustration shows that the smallest profit% in relation to turnover is within the Sales Department, which is reporting at 2%.

Now consider this scenario. If a franchise decides to increase its market share by selling more new vehicles, then the Sales department turnover will grow at a faster rate than the other departments. This means that more business will be conducted with the lower profit percentage rather than the higher profit percentages in the other departments. This means that it's simply a case of mathematics to understand why the business Net Profit% is falling and will continue to fall over the forthcoming years. When the department that has the largest turnover and the lowest profit grows at a faster rate than the other departments, there's only going to be one outcome; the business Return on Sales % is going to decline.

To add to this factor, the retail price of new vehicles usually increases year-on-year, dealer margins tend to be reducing and this is the area where the most growth is traditionally seen in a franchised dealership. Whichever way it is viewed, the Return on Sales % is fixed into a spiral of decline, but that is not always bad news.

By far, the more important key performance indicator to focus upon is Return on Funds Employed %. All trends are indicating that business profitability in terms of Return On Sales % will diminish, but the monetary value received may be higher. For instance, if 2% ROS equates to £200,000 and next year ROS % falls to 1.8%, which equates to £225,000, although the percentage has fallen, the *amount* of profit generated is higher.

A reducing ROS % means that companies will have to work harder by selling more products and services to generate this profitability. However, with business executives placing all their time and energy on diminishing ROS%, there is one critically important factor that is overlooked and not realised until it's too late...

When Return on Sales % enters a diminishing trend, this means that companies are handling more sales and generating lower profits and this means that companies require more Working Capital to keep running on a day-to-day basis. In other words, when

Return On Sales % falls, companies need more cash in order to survive, or they enter a condition called overtrading and they go bust.

When Return On Sales % is reducing, this should be a warning signal to re-assess the Working Capital to ensure that there is enough cash to survive the months ahead. The key performance indicator known as Current Ratio should have the focus because a business can survive without any profit, but it cannot survive without cash. *(See the Balance Sheet section of this book and page 199 of The KPI Book for more information on Current Ratio)*

In summary, Net Profit is the combined result of the actions in the departments and the ability to control the Overheads. Net Profit alone provides the final result, it does not state whether the company has done well or not because it's not possible to see if the company resources have been maximised in the accounting period; it's just a number.

If Return On Sales % is falling, success will be determined by the ability to manage cash flow and also to interpret the Profit and Loss Account to maximise company resources. Creating and maintaining the bridge between financial and commercial awareness is absolutely essential.

"I've made the tough decisions,
always with an eye toward the bottom line."

- Donald Trump

CHAPTER IV

HOW TO READ THE PROFIT AND LOSS ACCOUNT

"Results are important, but not nearly as important as knowing how you've achieved them."

- Jeff Smith

CHAPTER IV

HOW TO READ THE PROFIT AND LOSS ACCOUNT

Interpretation of the Profit and Loss Account is about gathering information to assess the strengths and weaknesses in operational performance. Once assessed, decisions can be made to implement tighter controls in some aspects of the business and set new goals and objectives in others.

The Profit and Loss Account is the window through which operational performance is viewed at all different levels and the more specific the information the better. However, with more information evident, the problem encountered is where to begin.

Understanding Cause And Effect
Cause and effect is about separating *actions* from *results*. Actions are causes and results are effects. Think about a learner driver for a moment. Imagine that a car is stationary at a junction in the road ready to turn right. The learner driver lets the clutch out too quickly and the car lurches forward faster than anticipated. The learner driver panics and grapples frantically with the steering wheel turning it quickly to gain control of the car.

The learner driver is dealing with the effects of their actions, not the causes. The cause of the car lurching forward is poor clutch control, but the learner driver tried to correct the problem by fighting the steering wheel. It doesn't matter how adept the driver becomes with the steering wheel, the problem will always exist as long as the driver has poor clutch control. The *cause* of the car lurching forward is poor clutch control and the *effects* are dealt with at the steering wheel. And so it is with the analysis of the Profit and Loss Account. Managers are so busy becoming adept with the steering wheel that they fail to gain control of the clutch. Cause and effect should be recognised in business analysis if corrective solutions are to be applied. If the results in the company are less than satisfactory then different actions are required to generate different results. It's not possible to change effects, it's only possible to change causes and the same effects will always be evident until the causes are changed. Becoming more adept at dealing with effects is counterproductive and energy sapping.

Whilst this may sound simple, in some cases cause and effect is the difference between financial and commercial awareness. Financial awareness provides the results, whilst commercial awareness provides the actions that generated those results. Understanding and recognising the difference between cause and effect is critical to proper interpretation of the Profit and Loss Account.

Getting Started

When most Managers receive their accounts, the first place that they look is the bottom line profit. The question must be, is this a good place to begin analysing the Profit and Loss Account or not? Let's consider the answers to this question by looking at it from different angles.

Assessing A Successful Result

When a Manager looks at the bottom line profit and they see that it's above budget or expectations, the Manager will feel happy inside knowing that they have achieved their objectives. They feel happy because they've achieved target but wait a moment... how likely are they to go back through the Profit and Loss Account to study, in depth, how they achieved this result? Would they feel contented with the result and simply glimpse over the statistics in the belief that everything must be running well because the result has been achieved?

Assessing A Poor Result

Now look from a different angle. The Manager receives the Profit and Loss Account and immediately looks at the bottom line profit. Unfortunately, they see that it's below budget or expectations, so what feelings are being experienced now? Feelings of happiness and achievement are certainly not evident; they are replaced with feelings of worry, stress and perhaps incredulity, but wait a moment... how will these feelings influence the thought processes of the Manager? In this state of mind, is the Manager more likely to go back through the Profit and Loss Account to study every single line to see where thing have gone wrong? Will the Manager be searching frantically for ways to improve performance?

The question here is, "Do the different emotions that are experienced with a good final result and a poor final result have any effect on the way that the Profit and Loss Account is analysed? The answer, of course, is a resounding yes and it's important to realise that in these two different cases, the Manager's emotions are influenced by "*effects*" and not "*causes*" and this approach to analysis leads to massive inconsistencies based on emotions and a career filled with stress.

The lesson to be learned here is that Profit is just an effect and to gain control of it, the causes must be accurately identified. If Managers look at the bottom line first, they will influenced by the emotion of the effect rather than the reality of the cause.

It's often been said by Managers that, *"It's natural to look at the bottom line first, especially if my wages are based on that figure."* Well, for the uninitiated, that may be true, but the bottom line is definitely not a good place to begin interpretation. However, someone could argue against this point by saying, *"I always look at the bottom line first to see if I've have achieved budget or not"*. Well, that's a complete fallacy because a budget does not consist of just the bottom line, does it? The budget is usually set up to mirror the Profit and Loss Account so that it's possible to compare each line of the results. Also, the bottom line profit isn't going to miraculously change just because Managers don't look there first, so why be negatively influenced by doing it?

The top performers in this area are objective. This means that they view their results without a predetermined agenda, without the handicap of heightened emotions that come with success or failure and they have the ability to separate actions from results.

When in possession of the Profit and Loss Account, the first question should not be, *"Have I hit budget or not?"* and then look straight at the bottom line. This is called a "bottom-up" strategy because thinking is developed from the bottom line, back up to the top of the accounts, but the problem is that it's ineffective.

Developing A Top-Down Strategy

When the Profit and Loss Accounts are received, begin with a question such as, *"Have we made the most of the resources that have been available to us?"* and then begin analysis at the top of Profit and Loss Accounts, working downward to the bottom.

When this top-down strategy is adopted by working through the sales volumes and Gross Profits of each individual product and service category that has been invoiced, a comprehensive understanding of the results is developed before being influenced by the bottom line, it's possible to see how well the products and services have been exploited within their marketplaces. Strengths and weaknesses will be identified and a realistic feel will be established between the results and the budget.

After these observations have been made, it's possible to move on to objectively assess the departmental expenses. Are there sufficient resources to deliver higher performance or is there a case to reduce resources and maintain steady growth?

By adopting this objective top-down strategy it's possible to instinctively know whether the bottom line profit is any good or not *before* it is seen because the person doing the interpretation will know if the resources have been fully exploited, irrespective of what is contained within the budget.

When applying the top-down strategy, it becomes more evident that each individual line of the Profit and Loss Account has its own specific part to play and with the correct identification of the performance *causes*, a little tweak in the right direction can make a big difference to the *effects* on the bottom line.

A "bottom-up" strategy usually results in randomly hacking away at expenses here and there, product discounting and knee-jerk reactions with little consideration, if any, for the overall outcome.

Managers using this strategy behave like learner driver struggling to keep control of the steering wheel when the car lurches forward, not realising that it's the clutch that's causing all the problems.

Looking at the bottom line first is no way to go about building solid foundations to achieve constant growth and success; the bottom-up strategy is used by the novice.

The top-down strategy produces clear understanding, objectivity and separates cause from effect. This is the strategy of the top achievers.

"Results are important, but not nearly as important as knowing how you've achieved them."

- Jeff Smith

CHAPTER V

HOW TO GET THE MOST OUT OF DEALER COMPOSITE

"The important thing is not to stop questioning. Curiosity has its own reason for existing."

- Albert Einstein

CHAPTER V

HOW TO GET THE MOST OUT OF DEALER COMPOSITE

Most franchised dealers are bound by the franchise dealer standards that require submission of the Management Accounts each month for entry into the manufacturers Composite.

What is Composite?
Composite or Inter Firm Comparison (IFC) is a document that is provided to franchised dealers by the manufacturer so that the dealers can measure their performance against other dealers who hold the same franchise. Every dealer submits their Management Accounts to the franchise on a monthly basis for input into the Composite and they are collated with every other dealer in the franchise and separated into groups for the purpose of performance comparison.

Composite is also used by the Business Development Team within each manufacturer so that they can assess the performance of each dealer and their network as a whole. The production of Composite is usually conducted by a third party company who specialise in collating data.

Composite grouping varies considerably between different franchises depending upon the number of dealers in the network, and the number of vehicles sold. However, the grouping process is usually determined by the New Vehicle Sales objectives, which is a common denominator among all dealers and could be structured as follows:

Group 1	Group 2	Group 3	Group 4
Up to 175	176 to 250	251to 400	401 +

As this table illustrates, Composite grouping in this example has no bearing on dealer profitability at any level, just sales volume expectations. Management Accounts for the whole dealer network are collated, dealers are separated into their various groups and the Composite reports are sent out to each dealer containing the comparative data.

When Managers and Accountants receive Composite, they can view their own dealer performance together with an average result of the group in which they are allocated. For instance, if a dealership has been assigned to group three, Composite would include the dealership's own figures together with the combined average of those dealers who have also been assigned to group three. In addition to that, statistics are calculated and provided for the combined averages of the group, the top performers in the group and the National Averages across the whole franchise dealer network. The averages of the top performers are usually called the "Upper Quartile" and represent the top 25% of the dealer network. Take care with analysis here because the upper quartile statistics are separate for each line, they are not usually the same dealer performance. For instance, Dealer A might be in the upper quartile for one area, but they might not be in the upper quartile for another area. Upper quartile statistics are independent of each other.

The first glimpse of a manufacturer's Composite can be more daunting than a full set of Management Accounts. However, manufacturer's Composites are no more complicated because they too follow the five basic steps. Composites only look more complex because there is more information on each step.

Does Composite Have Any Value?
There are some people who discredit Composite because the output of Composite does not match their own Management Accounts; it's probably a case of *"unfamiliarity breeds contempt"*.

One problem that exists is that a franchised dealer network consists of many different dealers who use different accounting software and there are different skill levels between Book Keepers and Accountants who input the data into the accounts and Composite. This means that there is often a degree of inconsistency in the structure of Management Accounts between each dealer. If the accounts are inconsistent between dealers, then Composite input will therefore be inconsistent. Some people claim that Composite is rendered useless because of the GIGO Principle: **G**arbage **I**n **G**arbage **O**ut.

Hopefully, if this book is embraced by dealers and manufacturers, the GIGO mindset and all of these problems with inconsistency will be eradicated and benchmarking will be more realistic and useful.

However, whilst these accounting inconsistencies are in existence, some Managers feel that it's difficult to compare individual figures with dealers within the same group, or indeed, on a national level, but this does not mean that Composite has no value. On the contrary, it's an awesome business tool when it's used correctly. The question is, *"How do you use Composite to gain the most advantage?"*

How To Take Advantage

The first thing to realise is that a manufacturer's Composite is not designed to be a replica of the dealers Management Accounts because there would not be any point in creating a duplicate document.

Composite takes the Management Accounts and produces key performance indicators (KPI) right across the whole of the business so that it's possible to compare those key performance indicators with other dealers and get a better understanding of what is happening in the industry.

Those people who discredit Composite by saying that it has no value because it's *"garbage in- garbage out"* are demonstrating to others that they do not understand the full power of key performance Indicators.

The critical factor for understanding Composite and understanding key performance indicators is about understanding *trends*. Here's an illustration to demonstrate this point:

Imagine that the national average for Net Profit is 2% and Dealership A is reporting a result of 3%. Should the dealership be pleased with that result?

Well, with other dealers reporting 2% and Dealership A delivering a result of 3%, most people would say,

"Yes, Dealership A has produced a good result". However, with a one-off snap shot like this, it's difficult to see the whole picture. Now let's add some trend information.

Trend 1: In Period 1, the result was 4% Net Profit, in Period 2 it was 3.6%, in Period 3 it was 3.2% and now in Period 4 the result is 3%.

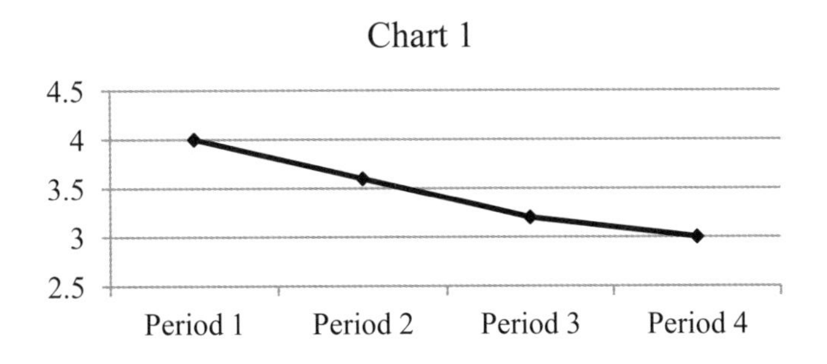

Trend 2: Now let's try trending the information in the other direction. In Period 1, the result was 2% Net Profit, in Period 2 it was 2.4%, in Period 3 it was 2.8% and now in Period 4 the result is 3%.

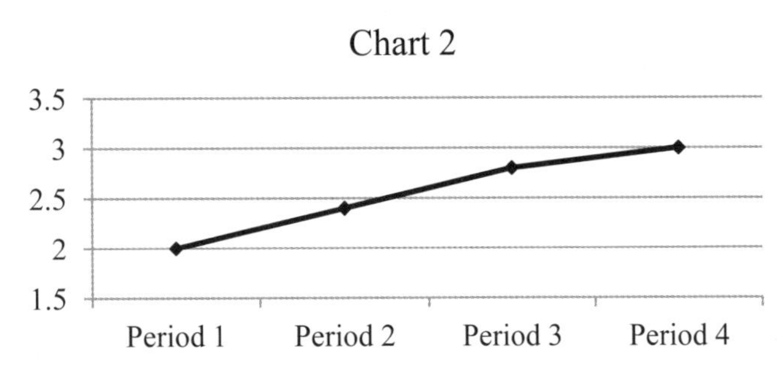

Should Dealership A be pleased with their result of 3% Net Profit with a national average of 2%, or do these different trends throw a different light on the subject?

The important factor in these two examples is that the initial result of 3% has not changed, but the trend leading up to the result changes everything.

If the results in Chart 1 were true and the trend fell from 4% to 3% Net Profit, the results would be devastating. However, if the results in Chart 2 were true and the trend increased from 2% to 3% Net Profit, everyone would be delighted.

Here's the evidence to confirm that interpreting a snap shot result is not always the best option because the real power of understanding lies in the trends.

The top performers in any industry will always study trends of key performance indicators so that the business direction is fully comprehended. The secret to selling more products and making more profit is about understanding trends and Composite is probably the best comparative trending document that is available to the franchised dealer.

This is where the garbage in, garbage out principle goes out of the window because it doesn't matter if different dealers input different information to produce inconsistencies because the *trend* of the key performance indicators will remain constant.

Understanding when and where a business activity is moving is what produces statistical value, not necessarily the snapshot result of an inconsistent figure.

Yes, the inconsistencies with accounting input will show up differences and anomalies in snapshot results, but that's not what Composite is designed to achieve. Composite is not a duplicate or a replacement for Management Accounts, it's a very powerful *trending* document to show movements within business activities.

A useful way to use Composite is to retain all copies and look for the information behind the trends that are of interest. Just looking at a single Composite may not be sufficient to achieve this because there may not be sufficient trend information.

A good Composite layout will contain a company summary with 12-month rolling averages on many of the most important key performance indicators so that trends can be seen month-by-month. These pages are perhaps the most useful to begin any analysis and then drill-down in the areas of performance that are of interest.

Composite is an enormously valuable asset in the armoury of business tools within a franchised dealership. It's a real benefit in bridging the gap between financial and commercial awareness because it provides many critical key performance indicators for the Motor Industry, the competition and the results of your own business. Discredit and ignore this powerful trending document at your peril.

"The important thing is not to stop questioning. Curiosity has its own reason for existing."

- Albert Einstein

PART II

UNDERSTANDING SALES, SERVICE, PARTS AND BODYSHOP

CHAPTER VI

THE DIFFERENCE BETWEEN PRODUCTS AND SERVICES

"There's only one thing worse than trying to run a business without any information and that's trying to run a business with the wrong information"

- Jeff Smith

CHAPTER VI

THE DIFFERENCE BETWEEN PRODUCTS AND SERVICES

Before going head first, straight into the departments, it's worth taking the time to understand that the accounting principles for each of the departments are not the same. This is to say that the accounting principles of the Sales and Parts Departments are essentially the same as each other and indeed, the Service Department and Bodyshop are essentially the same as each other, but the accounting principles in the Sales and Parts Departments are quite different to the accounting principles in the Service Department and Bodyshop.

Thankfully, the basic 5-steps remain in place across all four departments, so it's still very easy to understand, but there's a big difference at an operational level between buying and selling a product as opposed to buying and selling time and these differences must be captured accurately on the Management Accounts.

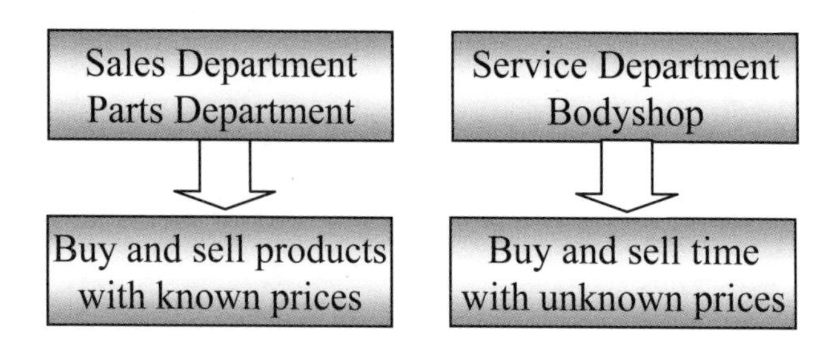

Buying And Selling Tangible Products

A business that buys and sells tangible products is relatively easy to manage and recording the Sales, Cost of Sales and Gross Profit is quite straight forward.

Here's a very simplistic and basic example for a business called Bakers Batteries. The business model is very easy to understand, they buy batteries at £10 each, they sell them at £40 each and they have departmental expenses of £25.

To get started, Bakers buy four batteries for stock at a cost of £10 each, which equates to £40. By the close of business they have sold one battery so their accounts for that period would look something like this:

Bakers Batteries Example 1

A) Sales	=	£40	(Sale of 1 battery)
B) Cost of Sales	=	£10	(Cost of the sold battery)
C) Gross Profit	=	£30	(A – B)
D) Gross Profit %	=	75%	(C ÷ A x100)
E) Dept. Expenses	=	£25	
F) Dept. Profit	=	£5	(C – E)
G) Dept. Profit %	=	12.5%	(F ÷ A x 100)
Stock value	=	£30	(3 batteries left in stock)

OK, that was nice and easy, wasn't it? Now let's redraw the accounts to see how different things would be if they had sold two batteries instead of just one. Remember that they begin with four batteries in stock.

Bakers Batteries Example 2

A) Sales	=	£80	(Sale of 2 batteries)
B) Cost of Sales	=	£20	(Cost of sold batteries)
C) Gross Profit	=	£60	(A – B)
D) Gross Profit %	=	75%	(C ÷ A x100)
E) Dept. Expenses	=	£25	
F) Dept. Profit	=	£35	(C – E)
G) Dept. Profit %	=	43.75%	(F ÷ A x 100)

Stock value = £20 (2 batteries left in stock)

Again, not too taxing on the brain, is it? Now let's take a look at the differences between these two examples because there are some very important things to consider here that often get overlooked.

A) Sales. Obviously, this has increased because the sales volume has increased.

B) Cost of Sales. Again, this has increased by the expected amount because the sales volume has increased. Two batteries have cost £20.

C) Gross Profit. Once again, no surprises because sales minus cost of sales is equal to £60. Sales and Cost of Sales has doubled, therefore the Gross Profit has doubled.

D) Gross Profit %. Here's a very important point to keep in mind. Although the monetary value of the Gross Profit has increased from £30 to £60, the Gross Profit % has remained constant. This is because the buying price and the selling price have also remained constant. This means that thc batteries that have been bought and sold have not exploited the market place any differently in both examples. Therefore we can conclude that when the sales volume of a product increases, it has zero effect on the Gross Profit %, *only the buying price or the selling price will affect the Gross Profit %.* Let the true operational effects of this action really sink in before reading on.

E) Dept. Expenses. These have not changed between the two examples because no other activity has been shown.

F) Dept. Profit. This has increased in example two, probably as expected because there is higher sales volume with no additional expense.

G) Dept. Profit %. This has increased significantly because the amount of Gross Profit has doubled and there have been no additional expenses.

Stock levels have fallen because more products have been sold from stock. The remaining batteries in stock can be sold at some point in the future; hopefully very soon.

As these two accounting examples demonstrate, buying and selling a tangible product is very simple and straightforward. The business buys some stock, sells it at a higher price than it was purchased for and what is left over, remains in stock to be sold another day. The secret to success is buying the right stock at the right price and selling it in its marketplace at a high price. The Gross Profit % is the KPI that reveals whether the business is exploiting those individual products in their marketplace or not. In its most basic form, this is how the Sales and Parts Departments operate with tangible products. However, the Service Department and Bodyshop is a different story altogether.

Buying And Selling Time and Services

The Service Department and Bodyshop are similar to each other, but completely different from the Sales and Parts Departments because they do not primarily sell products. Their primary functions are to buy a Technician's time and to sell the perceived value of the completed job. This change in business strategy has a major impact on the way that Management Accounts are structured, collated and interpreted.

One of the biggest areas of inconsistency in the Motor Industry is that some Management Accounts for the Service Department and Bodyshop do not recognise these major differences and they structure a Technician's time as though they are buying and selling a product; this is clearly wrong. Not only does this poor accounting practice produce inconsistency across the industry, but it also creates false results, which of course are much more damaging to the businesses concerned.

The obvious difference between buying and selling Products and Services is that products such as vehicles and parts can be held in stock for future use, but there is only one opportunity to make use of a Technician's time, it cannot be stored for later use; *"use it or lose it"* as the old saying goes.

When buying and selling tangible products, a business accumulates stock, but when buying and selling time, there is no stock. The Managers of the business must use the Technician's time when it is available to them during the normal working day, or it is lost forever.

Let's see how this stacks up when compiling Management Accounts for another simplified business model. Here's a basic example for a business called Raptor Repairs, who service and repair washing machines. The business model is very simple, they have one Service Engineer who is paid £10 per hour and they charge their customers £40 per hour for service and repair work. The department has expenses of £608.

In this particular period of time, the Service Engineer has been at work for 40 hours and he has been clocked onto jobs for 36 hours. The work that has been invoiced totals 42 hours. *(To keep things simple, no parts or sundries have been included).*

The Management Accounts for these transactions are shown on the next page. You can turn the page and look right now, or alternatively, you can obtain a pen and paper and assimilate the accounts for yourself and compare your reckoning with the results on the next page to test your financial and commercial logic.

Raptor Repairs Example 1

A) Labour Sales	=	£1,680	
B) Labour Cost of Sales	=	£360	
C) Labour Gross Profit	=	£1,320	(A – B)
D) Labour Gross Profit %	=	78.57%	(C ÷ A x100)
E) Idle Time	=	£40	
F) Dept. Expenses	=	£608	
G) Dept. Profit	=	£672	(C – E - F)
H) Dept. Profit %	=	40%	(G ÷ A x 100)

When most people are given an exercise like this, the Labour Sales and the Department Profit are usually the same as above, but the bits in the middle are usually different. From a financial viewpoint, it's OK to have the bottom line the same because it's mathematically stable, but from a commercial viewpoint, it the bits in the middle that illustrate what's happening at an operational level. Getting these bits in the middle correct is what makes the difference between a good business and a great one.

Working through the logic.
To have the ability to improve business performance, a Manager must have the ability to "see" the business activities reported in a financial context so that strengths and weaknesses can be identified, calculated and corrected back on the shop floor. Here's the logic for reporting a Technician's activity correctly.

A) Labour Sales.
Raptor Repairs charge their customers £40 per hour and 42 hours have been invoiced, therefore the Labour Sales = 42 hours sold x £40 = £1,680. This is the easy part.

B) Labour Cost of Sales.
Now this is where things get interesting and where most of the confusion and inconsistencies are caused within Service Departments and Bodyshops right across the Motor Industry. Let's look at the evidence and the different arguments that exist.

Raptor Repairs have a Service Engineer who is paid £10 per hour and works 40 hours; therefore the Service Engineers salary equates to £400. However, this is not the Labour Cost of Sales.

The Labour Cost of Sales is only equal to the cost of the time that the Service Engineer spent clocked onto jobs. If a Service Engineer is employed for 40 hours and only 36 of those hours are spent clocked onto jobs, then the Labour Cost of Sales is the cost of the 36 hours that were spent servicing and repairing.

Yes, the remaining 4 hours have to be paid to the Engineer as part of the total salary, but that is not part of the cost of production of the work that has been completed.

Think back to the example of Bakers Batteries where four batteries were purchased for stock and two of them were sold, the other two batteries remained in stock to be sold another day – here's the critical difference... *the Service Engineers time cannot be held in stock to be used another day, it's gone. Use it or lose it*

The Service Engineer was employed and paid to work for 40 hours but the Engineer was only deployed onto jobs for 36 of those hours. The remaining 4 hours at

£10 per hour still has to be paid to the Engineer, but what is that £40 for? Well, it's certainly not for the production of work, so therefore it's certainly not part of the Labour Cost of Sales. This is money that has been paid to the Engineer, but the company did not use this time and therefore it's an expense to the company; an unused resource.

In accounting terms, this expense is commonly known as Idle Time. This does not mean the Service Engineer was idle in the true meaning of the word, it means that the Service Engineer was employed to work, but for some reason, was not clocked onto jobs.

In this case, the Service Engineer's total salary is not seen on a single accounting line on the Management Accounts, it's separated onto different accounting lines so that the Manager can optimise the departmental performance in the future. Exactly the same is true for a Service Department and Bodyshop, so here's an example of where the Technicians salaries are distributed:

Technicians Salary Postings:
Labour COS = The amount paid to the Technician for the hours worked, this is the number of hours spent clocked onto jobs. Any bonus payments paid to the Technician should also be included here because the company is paying more money to produce its work.

Rectification = This is where a Technician has worked on a job, but the customer has returned with a problem. The Technician will need to clock onto this job with a new job card to rectify the problem, but the customer will not be charged again. This is an expense that needs to be closely monitored in li... with the company's right-first-time objectives because it's possible for a Technician to be efficient, but not very effective.

Idle Time = This where the Technician is in attendance at the business, but is not clocked onto jobs and is shown as an expense; it's a resource that has not been used. There are indeed many different reasons for the existence of Idle Time and it is one of the Manager's top priorities to keep this under control. Note that these are not unsold hours, but rather hours that have not been worked. The cost of Idle Time should be monitored closely and measured in line with the company objectives for Utilisation.

Holiday = This is where the Technician is not in attendance at the business and the company continues to pay the salary whilst the Technician is on holiday and is shown as an expense.

Sickness = This is where the Technician is not in attendance at the business and the company continues to pay the salary whilst off sick and is shown as an expense.

Training = This is where the Technician is not clocked onto jobs and is receiving training. This training may or may not be at the business, but represents the total cost, which is shown as an expense.

The Technician's salary is distributed across these different accounting lines so that the Manager can see where the company's money is being invested.

...d Services

...y has to pay the Technicians salary ... are working on jobs or not, so isn't it ... throw everything into the Labour Cost ...nting line?

Answer #1
Yes, from an accounting point of view it is *easier*, and that's probably why some Accountants do it that way, but the problem is that operationally speaking, it's completely worthless! That's because Managers cannot see where their companies are making and losing the money that's invested in Technicians and perhaps more importantly, the Managers cannot study the accounts and see how to improve the business in the future. And if that's not enough, if the salary is not apportioned correctly, it has the effect of a huge distortion on many of the critical departmental key performance indicators such as Utilisation and Productivity. The effects here are worse than running a business with a blindfold over the eyes... it means that Managers are developing future strategies for the company with information that is incorrect. You can't make a good decision with bad information.

Argument #2
This is all great in theory, but it sounds like hard work. How does all this information get from the Service Department and the Bodyshop into the hands of the Accountant?

Answer #2
The world of business is changing at an incredible rate and to keep pace with this change, the management team must be in possession of the right

information. The role of the Accountant within a business has changed. It's no longer acceptable for an Accountant or Book Keeper to remain seated in a remote accounts office crunching numbers and having no communication with the management team. It's also no longer acceptable for a Manager to believe or say, *"The numbers are for the Accountant to study, I don't need to understand them"*. Survival in business is about people working together with the right information and the right knowledge.

To survive and grow in our global economy, Accountants and Managers must work together to produce a set of Management Accounts that reflect what is happening at an operational level within the business and then both need to have the ability to do something with the information. As soon as one points the finger of blame at the other, it's game over for business development and the company enters the spiral effect.

Yes, it's more work, yes, it may be difficult at times and yes, you do have to do this if you care about the future growth and profitability of your company. If Accountants and Managers do not work in harmony together to produce figures that reflect operational performance, they will be giving the upper hand to other businesses in the marketplace who do work together to produce the correct information.

Gaining a competitive advantage does not begin by selling products and services cheaper than anyone else, it begins by having the correct information to develop the right strategy and then adapting quickly to the results and market forces.

If the Management Accounts are not structured so that operational performance is visible, the task of changing direction in business is nothing more than pure guesswork and the company's success is left to chance. It's like playing a game of darts with a blindfold over your eyes, if you're very lucky, you might hit the bull's-eye once, but you'll never do it on a consistent basis.

The accounting structure for buying and selling products is completely different to buying and selling a Technician's time and both accounting structures are evident in the Motor Industry, which can sometimes be very confusing to the uninitiated. The Sales and Parts Departments are of course "product based" with the Management Accounts being relatively easy to structure and straightforward to interpret. The Service Department and Bodyshop are "service based" businesses dealing with people's time, which is a much more complex structure, but this complexity brings with it highly accurate interpretation.

The difference in accounting between products and services is immense and if these differences are not clearly shown in the Management Accounts, the business runs free like a ship without a rudder.

The key to success is for Accountants and Managers to work together because the task cannot be completed by different people doing different things in different offices. Both need to be involved in the generation of the information to ensure it accuracy and both need to be involved in the development of business strategy.

As technology continues to develop, survival in business becomes more competitive each day and the key to success is having the right people in possession of the right information.

"There's only one thing worse than trying to run a business without any information and that's trying to run a business with the wrong information"

- Jeff Smith

Chapter VII

Understanding The Sales Department

"New vehicles come and go, used vehicles accumulate"

- Jeff Smith

CHAPTER VII

UNDERSTANDING THE SALES DEPARTMENT

This is a product based accounting structure and it doesn't matter whether a business is selling cars, bikes, trucks, boats power equipment, new or used vehicles, the basic principles of Management Accounts and the five-step structure is exactly the same for all products.

Reading this book could become very repetitive, tedious and boring if further explanations continued to separate cars, trucks, bikes, boats and power equipment, so from this point forward all of these products will be gathered under two collectives; New Vehicles and Used Vehicles.

New vehicles are of course the vehicles supplied to a business by the manufacturer or distributor, which are then sold to their customers. Used vehicles are those products that are taken in part-exchange or vehicles that are bought from customers, the trade or auctions and are subsequently sold onto customers as used vehicles.

Although new and used vehicles may reside in the same department and be under the responsibility of the same Sales Manager, they are in fact two separate businesses and should be treated as such within the structure of the Management Accounts.

New and used vehicles are affected differently by different market conditions and if the trend of those differences cannot be accurately identified, the business will be running blind. Sadly, the merging of information between new and used vehicles is commonplace and it's one of the main contributors for diminishing profitability in many franchised businesses. A lack of separation of these statistics results in a loss of clarity and effective business strategy. More speed in the wrong direction does not help, therefore this book strongly recommends that new and used vehicles are treated separately from each other.

Sales or Turnover

This is the monetary value of the vehicles that have been sold and invoiced in a given period of time and it is the value after discount has been given and does not include taxation. This is the same for both new and used vehicles.

Cost of Sales (COS)

This represents the amount of money that the company has paid to purchase the vehicles that have been sold and invoiced.

COS - New Vehicles: This represents the monetary value the company has paid to the manufacturer to purchase the new vehicles that have been sold and invoiced. Vehicles that been purchased, but not yet sold are classified as stock, not Cost of Sale.

Important note: The Cost of Sales should not include any expenses such as the Pre-Delivery Inspection (PDI) or commission payments to the

Sales Team, it is solely the purchase price of the new vehicle that has been sold. If any expenses are included here, the Gross Profit will automatically and *artificially* be reduced on each new vehicle, which loses the ability to assess new vehicle performance in their marketplaces.

COS - Used Vehicles: Methodology for ascertaining the Cost of Sales for used vehicles is completely different to the methodology for new vehicles. The Cost of Sales is established from the Stand In Value (SIV) of the used vehicle as opposed to its purchase price. This is because the effects of depreciation, back-end discounting and over-allowance need to be taken into account.

Back-End Discounting, Or Over-allowance

This is where a customer wants more for their part-exchange than it's worth to the company. For example, let's say that a part-exchange is valued at £6,000 but the customer wants £7,000 to do the deal on the new vehicle. In this case, the customer is provided with an over-allowance of £1,000 on their part-exchange; here's how it works:

When the new vehicle is handed over to the customer, the part-exchange becomes part of the company's used vehicle stock. The invoice shows a purchase price of £7,000 but the company values the vehicle at £6,000 which is known as the stand in value (SIV).

After the vehicle has been invoiced, the difference of £1,000 is taken from new vehicle Gross Profit and recorded as an over-allowance. This is known as a back-end discount because it's giving a discount to the customer in the form of an inflated part-exchange price which is then deducted from the new vehicle after the invoicing process. When this used vehicle is sold in the future, for let's say £9,000, in this case, the Cost of Sales is not the purchase price of £7,000, but the Stand In Value of £6,000.

Important note: The Cost of Sales for a used vehicle is derived from the Stand In Value and should not include any expenses such as reconditioning costs, refurbishment, valeting or commission payments to the Sales Team. The Cost of Sales for a Used Vehicle is solely the Stand In Value and nothing else.

If any expenses are included here, the Gross Profit will automatically and *artificially* be reduced on each of the used vehicles which loses the ability to assess used vehicle performance in their marketplaces.

The Reconditioning Argument

Some Accountants believe that Reconditioning Costs are part of the Cost Of Sales with the logic being that every used vehicle must be reconditioned therefore it's part of the Cost of Sales.

Looking at this from an accounting point of view, it makes no difference whether reconditioning costs are included or excluded because the bottom line will be the same. However, looking at this argument from a Sales Manager's point of view, it's not the result that matters, it's how you get there. The inclusion of Reconditioning Costs within the Cost of Sales will lower and distort the Gross Profit figure, which may lead to incorrect analysis. You can't make a good decision with bad information.

If Reconditioning Costs are included within the used vehicle Cost of Sales and the used vehicle Gross Profit is in decline, how could anyone conduct any meaningful analysis and endeavour to fix the downturn? Is the problem between the buying price and the selling price, which might relate to pricing strategies or selling skills, or is the problem related to Reconditioning Costs, which could be down to poor appraisals and all manner of other things. Merging refurbishment expenses within Cost Of Sales merges many different operational activities and is therefore considered to be poor accounting practice.

When Reconditioning Costs are included within the Cost of Sales, the power of analysis is lost because the Gross Profit key performance indicator has become corrupt. When changes are made to operational performance, the correct trend may not be witnessed.

If Managers and Accountants are to work together and tap into the power of understanding and separating cause and effect, then great care must be taken to separate the input to ensure that operational activities can be seen clearly. Reconditioning Costs are not part of the price that is paid for a used vehicle, it is an expense that is incurred *after* the vehicle has been purchased. The reconditioning cost itself is not charged by the person from whom the vehicle has been purchased, it's charged by a Service Department after the purchase has been conducted; it's a completely separate transaction.

To exact correct analysis on buying skills, selling skills and used vehicle appraisal, used vehicle

Reconditioning Costs must therefore be categorised as a departmental expense and not included within the Cost of Sale of the vehicle.

Gross Profit

This is a simple mathematical equation that takes the Sales or Turnover and deducts the Cost of Sales. Gross Profit is also expressed as a percentage of Turnover to give the Gross Profit% on each model that is sold.

Gross Profit - New Vehicles: Each manufacturer produces a range of vehicles of which some sell in higher volumes than others in the range and some are more profitable than others in the range. The Gross Profit% will therefore be different for each model derivative within the whole product range and Gross Profit% is provided to assess whether the company is exploiting each of these individual vehicles in their marketplaces. The amount of Gross Profit is different for each model in the range and different for each manufacturer and that's the reason why it is shown separately for each model derivative.

Gross Profit - Used Vehicles: Gross Profit here is calculated by taking the Sales or Turnover and deducting the Stand In Value (this may not be equal to the purchase price). Once again, the Gross Profit % may be calculated as a percentage of Turnover. In general, most Management Accounts and Composites do not report different categories of used vehicles as they do with new vehicles, with the odd exception being a separation between franchise and non-franchise vehicles; this is a major flaw.

A lot more could be done in this area with used cars being categorised by body type or price, used trucks could be categorised by weight, bikes could be categorised by sports, touring etcetera and power equipment could be categorised by all manner of different areas. If this degree of separation is not shown between the different categories of used vehicles, how will the Managers be able to track and trend which market sector is improving and which is in decline? Gut feelings and "hands-on" management is not enough because over a period of months, the human memory has a habit of weakening and then recreating its own version of what happened in the past. If the used vehicle business is to grow, clear separation of product grouping can only aid in the decision making process.

Finance & Insurance Income (F&I)
This is the revenue generated for the company by earning commission payments for arranging finance for customers and the selling of insurance-based products on their vehicles. This should not be merged into a single accounting line, it should be separated between new and used vehicles and shown in their respective departments because finance penetration on new vehicles is quite different to used vehicles.

Other Income or Miscellaneous Income
This is usually found on a manufacturer's Composite to allow the Accountant to include any products that the Sales Department has sold which are not included in the accounting lines of the Composite. For instance, the company's Management Accounts may have a line for Accessory Sales and the manufacturer's Composite may not have this line. In

this case, the revenues generated by Accessories would be posted to *Other Income* or *Miscellaneous Income* on the Composite. Again, this should be split between new and used vehicle departments.

Departmental Gross Profit

At a collective departmental level, it is impossible to ascertain any real meaning because different products sell at different prices and different volumes and the departmental Gross Profit simply merges them together to provide an average.

	Units	Sales	COS	GP	GP%
Model 1	15	129,780	128,483	1,297	1%
Model 2	6	59,070	58,125	945	1.6%
Model 3	12	151,824	150.611	1,214	0.8%
Model 4	27	404,892	396,390	8,501	2.1%
Sub Ttl.	60	745,566	733,609	11,957	1.6%
F&I		4,800	-	4,800	100%
Other		45,070	37,408	7,662	17%
Total GP		795,436	771,017	24,419	3.1%

In this simple illustration above, the Total Gross Profit adds up to 24,419 and is reported at 3.1% of Turnover, but if the other information was not listed above it, analysis would be impossible and the knowledge of how the result was generated could not be attained.

Departmental Gross Profit is not a useful measure because Gross Profit is an *individual product* measure. It ascertains whether each product is being exploited in its marketplace. The total information is required to illustrate business activity.

Manufacturers Bonus

These are bonus payments paid to the business by a manufacturer for the achievement of an objective which may or may not be related to sales volumes. Bonus payments can be earned on both new and used vehicles and can also be earned in two different ways:

1) New Vehicle Registration Bonus. A manufacturer usually issues some form of target-related earnings programme to each dealership in their network, which is based on new vehicle registrations (or warranty registrations) in a given period.

When the dealership registers the appropriate number of new vehicles to hit target, the bonus payment may be claimed from the manufacturer. This bonus payment should be posted on the accounts *after* the New Vehicle Gross Profit has been calculated because it is not guaranteed that the bonus will be achieved. Furthermore, if the dealership does achieve the target and claim the bonus payment, it is earned retrospectively and therefore does not change the buying price or the selling price of the new vehicles or any other products and services that have been sold. This is purely a bonus payment for the achievement of a target and should not distort Gross Profit because that would cause incorrect analysis.

2) New Vehicle Tactical Bonus. These bonus payments are quite different to the registration bonus because they are allocated to specific chassis numbers of vehicles.

From time-to-time, manufacturers may offer financial support for their slower-selling vehicles and this support is usually packaged in the form of a specific vehicle registration as opposed to the achievement of a number of vehicles being registered to hit a target.

This type of bonus payment is not linked with the target-related bonus payment, the terms provided are usually for a specific vehicle. For instance, a manufacturer might say, "*For every X model that the business registers, £500 bonus will be awarded.*"

This type of bonus payment is to assist with the sales volume of a specific model in its marketplace and the bonus payment should therefore be accounted for in the Cost of Sales because it actively *changes* the buying price of the new vehicle.

The specially selected new vehicles that contain the tactical bonus payment can then be sold at below the usual cost price with the *guaranteed* support or bonus payment without showing a loss on the Management Accounts. By placing this tactical bonus within the Cost of Sales and lowering the purchase price, the true trading position of the specific model is being shown and the Gross Profit is not falsely distorted.

3) Used Vehicle Bonus Payments

These payments are dependent upon the new vehicle manufacturer once again and bonus payments are usually targeted on the number of used vehicles purchased from the manufacturer in a given period of time. When achieved, this bonus payment should be posted on the accounts *after* the used Vehicle Gross Profit has been calculated because it is not guaranteed and it does not change the buying price of the used vehicles that have been purchased; it's just a bonus.

When volume bonus payments have been achieved, they can be found *after* Gross Profit and *before* the departmental expenses, which means that an additional accounting line is added. Alternatively, bonuses are sometimes shown as a negative expense.

Accounting For Manufacturer Bonus Payments

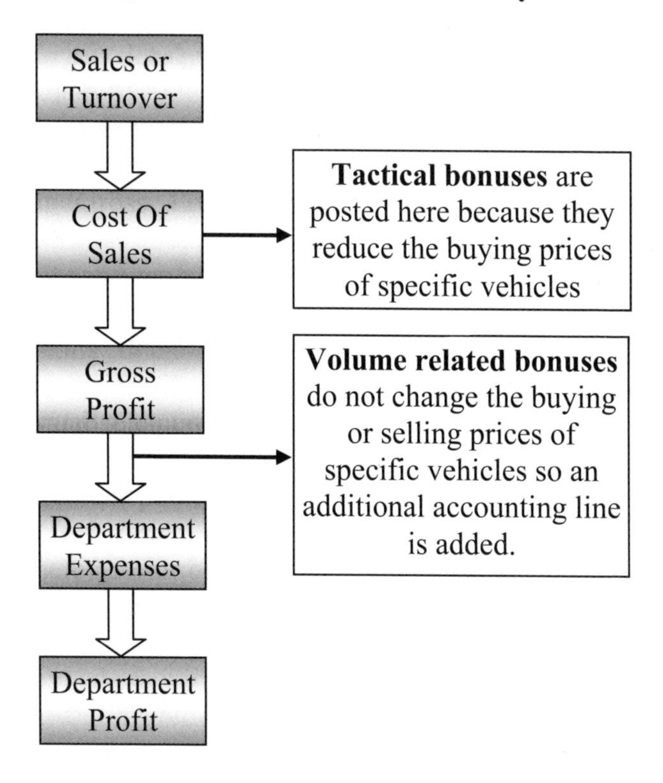

When any bonus payments are posted as negative expenses, this practice falsely reduces the expenses and distorts departmental analysis. This practice is not recommended because a potential problem within the departmental expenses may be overlooked and corrective action will not be undertaken.

The practice of posting all bonus payments for both new and used vehicles on a single accounting line is also not recommended. For correct analysis, bonus payments for New and Used vehicles should be split accordingly and shown separately in the respective new and used vehicle sales departments.

Sales Department Expenses

Departmental Expenses fall into two categories; those triggered by sales volume and those not triggered by sales volume. *Variable* or *Direct* are triggered by sales volume and *Semi-Fixed* or *Indirect* are not triggered by sales volume.

Variable Expenses or Direct Expenses

This section contains a comprehensive listing of the expenses that are triggered by sales volume. They are not listed in any order of importance, some Management Accounts may even list them in alphabetical order with no preference or priority so there's no need for concern about the order of the layout. The only important factors are that they are separated from the Semi-Fixed or Indirect Expenses and they are also separated between new and used vehicles so that accurate and meaningful analysis can take place. Let's take a closer look at some of the expenses that exist in this section.

Commission

This is the value of the commission payment made to the Sales People for the vehicles that have been sold and invoiced.

Any bonus payments made to the employees in the Sales Department for achievement of hitting any form of volume-related target are not to be included here because these bonus payments are not a direct consequence of the sale of the product. Volume related bonus payments are only paid when a target is achieved, whereas Sales Commission is paid on every product that is sold, regardless of target achievement.

Introductory Commission

This represents payments made to third parties or employees outside of the Sales Department for referrals made to the company which have resulted in a sale.

Delivery Costs

All costs associated with the delivery of vehicles to and from the company. This may include shipping and additional transports costs.

PDI and Plates

This expense is only applicable to new vehicles and includes the cost of preparation, number plates and safety inspections prior to delivery to the customer. This expense should not be included within the cost of sale of new vehicles.

First Service

This expense is quite rare nowadays because most manufacturers have abolished this service. However, it is still common in Motor Cycle manufacturers and is included in the On The Road price of the new bike.

When the customer returns to the supplying dealership to have the first service conducted, a set amount is usually taken from a provision which has already been taken from the new bike Gross Profit.

Where the customer takes the bike to a different business to have the first service conducted, the servicing dealer invoices the supplying dealer and there is usually an agreed fee within a dealer network for the work to be carried out.

Pre-Delivery Inspection
This represents the cost of a new vehicle going through the workshop to be prepared for the customer prior to delivery and handover. Some Accountants post this as part of the Cost of Sales of the new vehicle but this is considered as poor accounting practice because the Gross Profit on each new vehicle is instantly reduced which makes comparison with other businesses misleading. This is an expense and not part of the vehicle Cost of Sale.

Reconditioning
This represents the amount of money spent on used vehicles to refurbish them ready to retail. Once again, some Accountants post this as part of the Cost of Sales of the used vehicle but this is considered as poor accounting practice as explained earlier in this chapter.

To be successful with used vehicles, Managers need to accurately identify how good they are at buying and selling used vehicles and as a completely separate discipline, they need to know how good they are at controlling expenses.

These are three very different Sales Management activities and should not be bundled together and shown as a single figure in Gross Profit.

A good Accountant will have the ability to show the difference between Mechanical Reconditioning and Bodyshop Reconditioning; again two very different Sales Management disciplines. Body Reconditioning represents the money spent on body and paintwork on used vehicles; this could be sublet local repairs or work undertaken in the company's own Bodyshop. Mechanical Reconditioning represents the money spent in the Service and Parts Departments.

Reconditioning costs can escalate for many reasons including poor appraisal process of used vehicles, poor relationships between Sales, Aftersales and Bodyshop, lack of expense control, overage used vehicle stock and a host of many other reasons. Clearly, all of these factors must be isolated, controlled and not be *hidden* within the used vehicles Cost of Sales.

Sublet Cleaning

This represents the amount of money charged by an external valeting company for the cleaning of the new and used vehicles. External valeting companies usually charge on a per vehicle basis so it's relatively straightforward to show separation between new and used vehicles. Where the company employs its own valeting staff, those costs are not shown here.

Semi-Fixed Expenses or Indirect Expenses

This section contains a comprehensive listing of the expenses that are *not* triggered by sales volume. They are not listed in any order of importance, some Management Accounts may even list them in alphabetical order with no preference or priority so there's no need for concern about the layout.

The important factors are that these expenses are separated from the Variable or Direct Expenses and are also separated between new and used vehicles. However, in this section, the separation between new and used vehicles is not straightforward so the Accountant and Sales Manager may have to sit down together and agree a process of apportionment.

Example: If the Sales Department employs one Sales Manager who is paid a salary of £50,000 and is responsible for both new and used vehicles, then a decision must be made to share this salary between the two departments. It could be a straight 50/50 split or any other apportionment that is believed to be fair and equitable. There are no hard and fast rules or guidelines for this practice and apportionment will vary between different businesses.

Important Note: The principle of apportionment between new and used vehicle sales departments may apply to many of the other expenses in this section and it may be a practice that is not currently being used. However, it is absolutely necessary to create a meaningful used vehicle department, otherwise the new vehicle department will carry all of the expenses and the used vehicle department will not have enough information to be of any value.

Keeping these thoughts in mind, let's take a closer look at some of the expenses that exist in this section.

Bonus Payments

This represents all monies and incentives paid to staff for the achievement of a sales department target. This is not the same as a commission payment because a targeted bonus is only payable when the target has been achieved; it is not payable on each product sold as commission is paid.

Target-related bonus payments to staff could be shown as a separate accounting line or it could be included within the department salaries. The defining factor is simply to ask, how much information is required?

Computer Costs
This represents the money payable to computer maintenance contracts and equipment costs that are specific to the Sales Department. It may also include the cost of bespoke software agreements and franchise operating systems, subscriptions, maintenance agreements, but it does not include the development cost of web sites because that ought to be shown as a marketing expense. Once again, apportionment between new and used vehicles may be necessary.

Credit Card Charges
When customers pay a deposit using a credit card, the company will be charged a commission by the credit card company, which is around 2% of the transaction.

Taking a deposit on credit card is not usually a high value transaction, so credit card charges are minimal. However, taking payment for the total price of a vehicle with a credit card is considered bad practice. It is far less expensive to ask the customer to arrange a BACS transfer directly into the bank account or to use a Debit Card.

Demonstrator & Vehicle Running Costs
This represents the total operating costs and charges associated with the running of the vehicles that are in use by the Sales Department. Items here will include fuel, PDI charges, road fund licenses, tyres, accident repairs, scratch removal and servicing etc. Vehicle insurance is not shown here, that is shown within the company Overheads.

Demonstrator & Vehicle Funding
This is the cost of the borrowings incurred for demonstrators and all other vehicles that are in use within the new and used Sales Departments. This does not include the cost of funding used vehicle stock, just the vehicles that are in use.

Demonstrator & Vehicle Depreciation
Depreciation of demonstration vehicles has become a prominent concern for dealers as many manufacturers demand greater vehicle availability to enhance customer satisfaction. In addition to this, vehicles are depreciating at a greater rate than in previous times and this combination has seen depreciation rise out of all proportion causing major problems for many franchised dealerships.

There is no hard and fast ruling on how depreciation should be applied, but some manufacturers do provide guidelines. In general terms, some Accountants apply depreciation at a flat of between 2% and 5% per month, whilst other may apply a monetary sum per vehicle each month. Of course these percentages and monetary figures are for example only, the true cost of depreciation is wholly dependent upon the specific vehicles and the franchise held.

The cost of depreciation on demonstration vehicles has traditionally been the subject of conflict and controversial debate between the franchised dealer and manufacturer; dealers say, *"We need more financial assistance to help with this rising cost"* and manufacturers say, *"Depreciation on demonstrators is a cost of the franchise"*. It's a debate that set to continue for the foreseeable future.

Although costs are escalating in this area, one thing must be understood...if demonstration vehicles are not depreciated sufficiently and priced attractively, they will not sell and the company will be left with cash tied up in too many, over-age and over-priced vehicles. It's a bitter pill to swallow and an expense that must be tightly controlled.

General Expenses or Miscellaneous Expenses

This line usually appears at the bottom of the list of expenses to capture uncategorised items. It's a dangerous expense line to have in a set of Management Accounts because it contains expenses that are not separately categorised in any other expense and therefore they can become invisible if left unchecked.

This expense line is always evident on the manufacturers Composite and it needs to be there because it has to provide a "*Catch-All*" facility for the expenses that may be individually itemised on a dealer's Management Accounts but may be separately itemised on the Composite. If the Accountant is faced with this dilemma and is unsure where to post a particular expense, it usually gets posted here; it's for those expenses that cannot be easily allocated to another expense line. If this expense is evident on the Management Accounts, the Sales Manager must work closely with the Accountant to ensure that everything that is posted to this account is correct, agreed and tightly controlled. Failure to do so could result in a loss of profits without any understanding of why it's happening.

Marketing

This is the cost of all advertising and marketing initiatives for the sales departments including new vehicle brochures, but less any marketing support provided by the manufacturer. This expense is sometimes easy to separate between new and used vehicles, but there are other occasions where apportionment may have to take place; the cost of the company web site or a combined new and used vehicle advertisement for instance.

Marketing for both new and used vehicle is a major expense and should be separated and shown in the appropriate department. Failure to do so will usually result in the entire marketing expense being shown in the new vehicle department with nothing being shown in the used vehicle department. This is considered to be poor accounting practice because analysis of the different departments is not possible. You can't make a good decision with bad information.

NI & Pension

In countries where National Insurance (NI) and pension payments are made for employees, these expenses are shown separately to the basic salaries and sales commissions so that a fair and realistic comparison on salaries can be made.

Petrol

This relates to all fuel types including diesel of course and represents the monetary value of the fuel provided for sold vehicles.

Some dealers provide a full tank of fuel in every vehicle that is sold, others do not. Different companies have different views on how much fuel is provided for customers' vehicles and the effects upon Customer Satisfaction, nevertheless, it is an expense that must be monitored closely. As with all expense control, there is a fine balance between Customer Satisfaction and cost reduction.

Policy Adjustment (New and Used)

This expense is known by many other names including, Policy, Policy Grant, Rectification, Late Costs, Goodwill and Further Work After Sale to name but a few.

It occurs when a vehicle has been sold and delivered to the customer and the customer returns to the Sales Department with a problem on the vehicle; now a decision must be made:

Decision 1: The Sales Manager could explain that the fault is outside of the warranty terms and conditions and ask the customer pay to rectify the fault. There would not be any expense to the Sales Department here, but depending on the fault and length of time that the customer has had the vehicle, a decision like this may have serious ramifications and further implications upon Customer Satisfaction. It is for the Sales Manager to decide upon this delicate balance.

Decision 2: Alternatively, the Sales Manager may decide to accept the customer's concerns with the vehicle and agree to rectify the problem with no cost to the customer. After a discussion with the Service Manager, it is agreed that it is not a fault that should have been rectified by the Service Department before the vehicle was handed over to the customer, the fault is not covered by the vehicle warranty and therefore the cost of rectifying the fault falls to the Sales Department.

Where this is the case, the vehicle is rectified in accordance with the Sales Manager's agreement, the invoice for the repair is issued to the Sales Department and it is posted here under Policy Adjustment (or whatever name used on the accounts).

A question that is often asked is, *"Why is this expense in the Semi-fixed or Indirect section as opposed to the Variable or Direct Expenses because it is triggered by sales volume – the more vehicles you sell, the more the rectification?"*

Well, the reason that it's in this section is because this expense is not applied to *every* vehicle that is sold (like commission for instance), it's only evident on a few of the vehicles that are sold that develop a fault.

However, the higher the sales volume the greater the propensity, or the higher the likelihood that more of these faults will be evident, but Policy Costs are not a consequence of every vehicle sale and it's for the Sales Manager to decide whether to pay them or not. This expense is therefore not a direct consequence of selling a vehicle.

Stock Maintenance
This is the cost associated with maintaining new and used vehicles that are on display or in storage. Inevitably, vehicles get damaged from time to time and have to be repaired and these costs are shown here. This is not to be confused with individual vehicle rectification or pre-delivery Inspections; it's an expense for the maintenance of the stock as a whole.

One example might be where contract cleaners are commissioned to wash the used vehicle stock every few days. (This would not be the case if the company employs cleaners.)

Stock Write Down
Anyone who buys and sells used vehicles will know all too well that used vehicles suffer the consequences of depreciation and values diminish on an ongoing basis.

This expense is to show the value of depreciation that has been allocated to used vehicles, which has the effect of reducing the Stand In Values of the used vehicle stock to reflect the market conditions. There is no industry standard for depreciating or writing down used vehicles, but there are various different methods in use:

A) Stock Value Adjustment: This is a system where the Accountant applies a percentage across the whole used vehicle stock value to arrive at a depreciation figure each month, whilst others may prefer to apply a fixed monetary value rather than a percentage each month.

Neither of these methods accurately assesses the true rate of depreciation in the used vehicle stock, but they do provide a monetary figure so that the Sales Manager can share or distribute the depreciation figure across different models that are in stock. This value of depreciation is apportioned on the basis of the Sales Manager knowing and understanding the local used vehicle marketplace. The amount of depreciation calculated may be enough to account for a realistic adjustment, but then again, it may not. These methods of depreciation simply create a value to work with each month.

B) The Fixed Rate: This system is a little less flexible than others and it operates with the Accountant applying a fixed amount of money per vehicle, regardless of the rate of depreciation of each vehicle. The Sales Manager has no input in this system and does not decide how the total amount of depreciation is distributed across the stock. Each vehicle is written down by a fixed sum each month. Once again, this system does not take into account the true position of depreciation; it's just an accounting principle that's used to arrive at a figure for depreciation.

C) Book Adjustment: This system is where a company assesses each vehicle on an individual basis and writes them down to Industry Guide values. Neither the Accountant nor the Sales Manager have any direct input on the value of depreciation that is allocated and the depreciation figure is more realistic, but it can vary wildly each month and is subject to change with seasonality. Although it is more realistic than other systems, it is far more unpredictable as it relies upon industry guides rather than local knowledge.

D) No Action: Some companies choose not to depreciate used vehicles and adopt the attitude that someone will buy the vehicles at sometime; even if that happens to be over a year later. This is considered to be poor practice because there is no pressure on the Sales Manager to dispose of any overage vehicles and in addition, the company will not be able to take advantage of the corporation tax relief.

In summary, it's a fact that used vehicles depreciate and this expense shows the value of the depreciation each month. The value of depreciation is then deducted from the used vehicle Stand In Values so that the stock value is maintained at realistic levels. This expense is not to be confused or amalgamated with the depreciation of demonstrators; that should be shown on a separate accounting line.

Stocking Charges – New Vehicles

This represents the interest charges that are levied on new vehicles that are held in stock. Fortunately, franchised dealers do not have to pay outright for their new vehicle stock because most manufacturers have an associated finance company that provides a credit facility specifically for this purpose; this credit facility is usually called a Floor Plan. Each manufacturer sets the terms and conditions for their own Floor Plan and most operate in similar ways.

New vehicles are supplied and delivered to the franchised dealership on a Consignment basis. This means that the dealership has a specified period of time where it pays only the interest on the new vehicles and when the specified time limit expires, the dealer must then pay for the new vehicle in full; full payment of a vehicle is known as Adoption. Typical consignment terms for the Floor Plan might be:

New vehicles in stock between 1 to 30 days may be Interest free. New vehicles in stock between 31 – 180 days may incur interest charges at a specified rate. At 181 days in stock, the new vehicle comes off the Floor Plan and must be adopted, which means that the dealer must pay in full for the vehicle.

When a new vehicle is sold and registered, no matter what age in stock, the vehicle comes off the Floor Plan and must be paid for in full.

This is a generic example of how a Floor Plan operates and each manufacturer will stipulate their terms and conditions and it is only the interest charges that are accumulated that are shown in this expense, not the value of the new vehicle stock.

Note: It is considered poor practice to possess any adopted stock because it ties up the company's cash unnecessarily. All new vehicles should be sold within the consignment period to avoid adoption.

Stocking Charges – Used Vehicles

This is the expense that captures the interest charges on used vehicle stock and it works in a completely different way to a new vehicle Floor Plan.

Finance companies offer a credit facility on used vehicles that allows the dealership to pay the interest charges only without having to provide the funds for the used vehicle stock. Each finance company will have their own terms and conditions for this credit line, but they too operate in similar ways.

Each month, a representative from the finance company will visit the dealership and conduct a physical check of the used vehicles in stock. Each vehicle is valued by using the industry guides and a valuation is therefore ascertained for the whole stock, this may be different to the company's stock valuation. The finance company will provide a credit facility which is usually up to 80% of the stock valuation that has been ascertained. The dealership will pay interest to the finance company on the money borrowed and that interest charge is shown here on this expense line.

In the case where the company does not utilise a credit facility from a finance company, alternative funding must be sourced with the most common being the Bank Overdraft. In this case, it may be difficult to separate the interest charges for the used vehicle stock from the total bank charges and so one of two things may happen here;

1) Interest charges are not shown here, they remain in the total interest charges in the company Overheads

2) Notional interest charges are levied here and the amount is deducted from the company Overheads.

If we continue with the maxim, *"Results are important, but not nearly as important as knowing how you've achieved them"* then some may argue that the better route would be to show interest charges for the used vehicle stock, even if those charges are notional, because the Sales Manager can then see the cost of the borrowings, rather than ignoring them or being blissfully unaware. Whichever route is chosen will have an impact upon the bottom line of the department so when comparing results with others, it's important to know if used vehicle stocking charges are shown here or not.

Salaries & Wages
This represents the basic wages of the personnel in the Sales Department which will include the Sales Manager's salary and any Administration staff. It will also include the basic salaries of the Sales People, but it will not include sales commission payments. Also excluded from here is National Insurance and Pension which has its own accounting line where applicable.

Storage Charges
This represents the charges for storing vehicles in compounds and any other off-site storage facilities.

Subscriptions
This represents fees and subscriptions payable to industry journals, magazines, used vehicle valuation guides, governing bodies, and trade bodies.

Training
This represents the cost of training for the whole department which includes the cost of the attendance, overnight accommodation, travel and subsistence.

Direct Profit
This is also known as Departmental Profit, Operating Profit or more colloquially, the bottom line. This is a

simple mathematical equation, which is calculated by taking the total Departmental Gross Profit, plus any bonus where applicable, minus all Departmental Expenses. Operationally speaking, it is of course an "effect" rather than a "cause" therefore it can only be influenced by other operational factors.

As stated in Chapter IV, it's pointless beginning the analysis of the department here because there's so much information that goes into it. Proper analysis of the department examines this figure last of all because it is the understanding of the individual components that make up this figure that unleashes the real power of performance improvement.

Many Management Accounts will illustrate this figure as a percentage of Turnover but it is always the trend of this Key Performance Indicator that is of primary importance.

Example:

(A) Direct Profit	=	£97,208	
(B) Departmental Turnover	=	£3,240,233	
(C) **Direct Profit %**	=	**3%**	(A ÷ B x 100)

Knowing how to calculate the Direct Profit percentage is one thing, but knowing how to influence the trend is what is really required and that information is gleaned from the true understanding of both financial and commercial awareness.

To derive the most performance gain in both new and used vehicles, Management Accounts need to be split into different departments and therefore the Direct Profit for each department will be shown separately rather than being merged. The businesses of new and used vehicles operate in completely different ways with very different market forces and the results of one department should not mask or enhance the performance of the other. If the two departments are merged in any way, some operational shortfalls will become invisible and performance gain throughout the Sales Department will be extremely difficult to achieve.

The key to success with improving operational performance with used vehicles is to understand the relationships between Direct Profit, Circulation of Investment, Stock Turn, Return on Investment and to have the ability to accurately forecast how these key performance indicators will change before new initiatives are implemented. Used vehicles are the key to success, if you can't sell used vehicles, you won't sell new vehicles.

"New vehicles come and go,
used vehicles accumulate"

- Jeff Smith

CHAPTER VIII

UNDERSTANDING THE SERVICE DEPARTMENT

"The only people who have the ability to change and seek improvements are those who want to, and not everyone wants to."

- Jeff Smith

CHAPTER VIII

UNDERSTANDING THE SERVICE DEPARTMENT

The Service Department is completely different from the Sales Department because its primary function is to "buy and sell time" as opposed to buying and selling tangible products. This change in business strategy has a major impact on the way that Management Accounts are structured, collated and interpreted. Before reading this chapter, please read Chapter VI because the differences in the accounting structures are explained in detail throughout.

Part 1 - The Basic Business Concept

A business employs a Technician for a given amount of time with an hourly wage rate. For the sake of simplicity, let's keep this example to one Technician who is employed for 8 hours per day, five days per week, with a salary of £10 per hour. It is the task of the business to have the Technician working on vehicles during the time that he is at the business and to sell the perceived value of the service or repair to its customers in order to make a profit.

Note: It is not the Technician's time that is being sold to the customers, it is the "perceived value" of the service or repair that has been carried out. That's something quite different because the perceived value can often be a higher time value than the Technician has spent working on the service or repair of the vehicle.

Part 2 - The Basic Terminology

The companion to this volume, The KPI Book, deals with this area much more succinctly, but for this chapter, the following terminology is in use:

Hours Bought: The total number of hours that the business will pay to the Technician, which includes time at the business, Holiday, Sickness and Training.

Hours Attended: The total number of hours that the Technician is at the business and available to work on vehicles. This excludes Holiday, Sickness and Training.

Hours Worked: This is the total number of hours that the Technician spends clocked onto jobs, spanner-in-hand, working on vehicles.

Idle Time: This is the total number of hours that a Technician is at the business, but is not clocked onto jobs. (Hours Attended minus Hours Worked.)

Hours Sold: The total number of hours that are invoiced to customers.

Recovery Rate: The amount of money that a customer is charged for each hour that has been sold.

Wage Rate: The amount of money that the business pays to the Technician for every hour of employment.

All of these hours are captured and coded separately on the Management Accounts so that accurate and meaningful interpretation of the figures and key performance indicators can be undertaken.

Part 3 – The Basic Structure

Now let's take a look at some activity for a simplified business called *Magnum Motors* and set up the Management Accounts to reflect what's happening in the business. This models simply examines labour, other sales such as Oil will be discussed later.

Magnum Motors Business Activity:

A) Hours Bought	=	160
B) Hours Attended	=	140
C) Hours Worked	=	126
D) Hours Sold	=	150
E) Recovery Rate	=	£95
F) Wage Rate	=	£10
G) Other Expenses	=	£6,950

Before you continue reading, cover up the example on the adjacent page, take a pen and piece of paper and create a very simple set of Management Accounts to represent these statistics. Once you've finished, you can compare your results with the example overleaf and as you continue reading, you can compare your thinking with the answers and logic that's provided throughout the rest of this chapter.

Remember at all times, that this structure is very different from selling a tangible product, it's selling the value of a service or repair with the cost of the Technicians time to complete the tasks in hand.

The following example illustrates how the Management Accounts need to be structured in order to reflect what is happening with labour only at an operational level within the Service Department:

Example 1: Management Accounts Structure for Magnum Motors

A) Hours Bought	=	160	
B) Hours Attended	=	140	
C) Hours Worked	=	126	
D) Hours Sold	=	150	
E) Recovery Rate	=	£95	
F) Wage Rate	=	£10	
G) Other Expenses	=	£6,950	
H) Labour Sales	=	£14,250	(D x E)
I) Labour Cost of Sales	=	£1,260	(C x F)
J) Labour Gross Profit	=	£12,990	(H – I)
K) Labour Gross Profit %	=	91.16%	(J ÷ H %)
Expenses:			
L) Idle Time	=	£140	(B – C x F)
M) Holiday, Sickness Etc	=	£200	(A – B x F)
N) Other Expenses	=	£6,950	
O) Total Expenses	=	£7,290	(L + M + N)
P) Department Profit	=	£5,700	(J – O)
Q) Department Profit %	=	40.00%	(P ÷ H %)

Now let's follow the maths and logic on each of these accounting lines.

H) Labour Sales

This represents the amount of money that customers have been charged for the "labour only" content of the service or repairs that have been invoiced. It does not include the cost of any parts that may have been charged to the customer; where applicable, Parts Sales will be shown and itemised separately. Note that the Recovery Rate is after any discount that may have been applied.

Using the *Magnum Motors* business example, the value of the Labour Sales amounts to £14,250 which equates to the number of hours that have been sold to customers multiplied by the Recovery Rate, (D x E).

From an accounting point of view, it's very simple to show this on the Management Accounts, but from a Service Management point of view, it's really not much use because the Manager needs to know where and who the Labour is being sold to so that strengths and weaknesses can be identified. It is for these reasons that on most sets of Management Accounts, the Labour Sales are separated, at the very least, into three basic categories:

Retail Labour Sales = (General public, companies)
Internal Labour Sales = (Sales Department)
Warranty Labour Sales = (Franchise Warranty)

As businesses grow and evolve, additional accounting lines may be added to show where the Labour Sales are coming from such as MOT, Budget Servicing, and Repair and Maintenance Contracts to name but a few. The more clear the separation between categories that is shown, the more accurate the interpretation can be. These additional accounting lines do not change the complexity of the Management Accounts, in fact the opposite is true, additional information makes the business revenues easier to understand.

Important note: The number of hours sold to the customer and the amount of money charged for each hour sold is not decided or dictated by the Technician. In other words, "*Technicians do not sell hours*", that's the job of the Service Receptionist or Invoicing

Clerk. The number of hours sold on the customers invoices can be higher or lower than the time it's taken the Technician to complete the work. From an operational management point of view, there may be some time guidelines in place for the Technician to complete the work, but from an accounting point of view there are no "*absolute*" links between the length of time that the jobs have taken and the number of hours that are sold to the customers.

In summary then, Labour Sales simply represents the amount of money that customers have been charged by the Service Receptionist or Invoicing Clerk for the labour-only content of the Service Department invoices. It's influenced by their selling skills when booking-in work and explaining the invoices to customers; Technicians do not *sell* hours, they *work* hours.

Labour Cost of Sales

As explained in detail in Chapter VI, this is the section that causes the most confusion and complete chaos across the whole of the Motor Industry. Let's take a look at the *Magnum Motors* example to understand the logic that's in place here.

A) Hours Bought	=	160	
B) Hours Attended	=	140	
C) Hours Worked	=	126	
D) Hours Sold	=	150	
E) Recovery Rate	=	£95	
F) Wage Rate	=	£10	
G) Other Expenses	=	£6,950	
H) Labour Sales	=	£14,250	(D x E)
I) Labour Cost of Sales	=	£1,260	(C x F)

The example shows Labour Sales are £14,250, but the question that remains is, "How much did it cost *Magnum Motors* to produce that value of Labour Sales?"

The Labour Cost Of Sales is equal to the hourly rate paid to the Technicians (the wage rate) multiplied by the time it's taken the Technicians to complete those jobs, which is known as the Hours Worked. Therefore the Labour Cost of Sales is £1,260 (C x F). Note that this is not the Technicians total salary, it represents only the portion of the Technicians salary that was paid for producing the hours that have been sold. The remainder of the monies paid to Technicians such as Idle Time, Holiday, Sickness and Training will be discussed in more detail later in the chapter.

In order for the Labour Cost of Sales to be collated accurately, the Technicians must be clocking on and off job cards and the Hours Worked must be accurately recorded on the Dealer Management System. Where automated electronic systems are not in place, the Hours Worked must be given to the Accountant by the Service Manager; communication in either case is critical to ensure the accuracy of the output.

Common Accounting Errors

The most widespread inconsistencies appear when the Accountant and Manager do not communicate on such matters and the input varies wildly across the industry. Here are some typical examples:

Error #1- The Labour Cost of Sales is equal to the hourly rate paid to the Technicians (the wage rate), but only whilst the Technicians are present at the business, which is the Hours Attended. Therefore the Labour Cost of Sales in the Magnum Motors example would be equal to £1,400 (B x F).

This methodology is incorrect because Idle Time would have to be reported at zero, which of course is operationally impossible. In addition to this, the Labour Gross Profit percentage would be changing after every hour had been sold because the labour cost of sales would remain constant; this would render any daily operating control completely useless. Also this methodology would have a significant effect upon Utilisation because it would have to be reported at 100%, which renders the Manager blind to any issues surrounding workshop loading. Since Utilisation is the biggest profit builder in the Service Department, it obviously places the company in a disadvantageous position to have the accounts structured in this way. The Labour Cost of Sales is therefore <u>not</u> equal to the amount of money paid to the Technicians for the Hours Attended.

Error #2 - The Labour Cost of Sales is equal to the Technicians total Salary. The argument put forward here is, *"The business has to pay the Technicians' total salary whether they are at work, on holiday, off sick or doing training so the whole of their salary is the Labour Cost of Sales."* In this instance the Labour Cost of Sales in the Magnum Motors example would be equal to £1,600 (A x F). This methodology is also incorrect because it includes all of the problems listed in error #1 and it also corrupts things even further by including the cost of Holiday Sickness and Training thereby disguising any potential problems that may exist with Technicians absenteeism. The Labour Cost of Sales is therefore not equal to the Technicians total salary.

Error # 3 – This is not an accounting input error, but rather a management interpretation error. Some Managers believe that the Labour Cost Of Sales is equal to the hourly rate paid to the Technicians (the wage rate) multiplied by the number of Hours Sold because that's what has been invoiced to the customer and that's how some Technicians earn their bonus. In this case the Labour Cost of Sales in the Magnum Motors example would be equal to £1,500 (D x F). This methodology is also incorrect and is not part of any standard accounting practice; it's simply a misconception in interpretation that some Managers get drawn into.

Operational Strength and Vision

Yes, it can be argued that these so called errors are mathematically stable and from an accounting point of view they may be deemed as correct, but the problem is that these methods leave the Manager blind to all operational performance because it's not possible to see what is happening on the workshop floor. If the Management Accounts do not provide that clear vision for the Manager, they are worthless.

There are many other permutations for what is and what is not included within the Labour Cost of Sales and whilst there may be sound logic behind each of the methodologies, from a Service Management point of view, there is only one way to make operational performance visible and controllable and that is to have the Labour Cost of Sales equal to the money that is paid to the Technicians for the number of Hours Worked. This is because it is the Hours Worked that represents the true cost of the Hours Sold and both can be controlled at an operational level by the Manager.

What about Technicians' Bonus Payments?
Not all Service Departments have a bonus scheme in place for Technicians and for those that do, there are many different bonus schemes and many different ways of rewarding Technicians for a job well done.

Where a Technicians' bonus scheme is in place, it is usually based on the enhancement of production in some way and therefore any bonus payments made to Technicians is increasing the cost of the Hours Worked as opposed to increasing the cost of Idle Time, Holiday Sickness and Training.

In this case, bonus payment increases the cost of the Hours Worked to the company and therefore the entire bonus payment should be included within the Labour Cost of Sales. So to have a little more clarity, the definition is extended to:

Labour Cost of Sales is equal to the money that is paid to the Technicians for the number of Hours Worked, which is to include all bonus payments.

What about Technicians' Overtime Payments?
This is quite simple to understand because the rules of accounting are the same. Firstly, let's define exactly what Overtime actually is. This is where a Technician is required to work outside of normal working hours and is usually paid at a higher hourly rate.

Let's say that a Technician attends 10 hours Overtime and is paid £12 per hour as opposed to the normal £10 per hour. The Technician must still clock on and off job cards whilst working Overtime and it is the Technicians time that is spent clocked onto jobs that determines the Hours Worked, which makes up the Labour Cost of Sales. The hours of Overtime that are not clocked onto jobs are classed as Idle Time. To summarise, the treatment of Overtime is exactly the same as for normal working hours, the only difference being that Overtime is usually paid at a higher hourly rate. The effect of Overtime is that the Labour Gross Profit percentage will be reduced because the Labour Cost of Sales is now higher due to the company paying the higher Overtime rate for the Hours Worked.

Whilst working Overtime, there will undoubtedly still be a small element of Idle Time and this should be recognised as such and speaking from a Service Management point of view, the company should not be embarking upon any Overtime if Utilisation is anywhere near or below 95%.

What About Work In Progress?

This is where work has been carried out or part carried out on vehicles but the job cards have not been completed. In other words, Technicians have worked on jobs and those jobs have not been invoiced as yet.

When Work In Progress (WIP) is allowed to increase the effects are that the Hours Worked will increase, but the Hours Sold will not, which means that the Labour Cost of Sales will increase in value but the

Labour Sales will not. This causes a lower value to be reported in Labour Gross Profit and also the Labour Gross Profit percentage will be reduced because the Labour Sales are not reported but the Labour Cost of Sales are reported.

In addition to this distortion, high levels of Work In Progress will have a significant effect on key performance indicators. Utilisation will be seen to increase because the Hours Worked are being recorded but Productivity will be seen to decrease because the Hours Sold are not being recorded.

One critical error in handling Work in Progress is for the Hours Worked that relate to the Work In Progress to be carried forward into the next month when the jobs are invoiced. This action would show a high decline in Utilisation in the month that they were moved from and a high increase in Utilisation in the month that they were carried to. In such a case it is possible for Utilisation to be reported in excess of 100% , which is operationally impossible because that would mean that Technicians are clocked onto jobs when they are not attending the business. One of the arguments for conducting this practice is for calculating Technicians bonus payments when a time-saved bonus scheme is in place, which is calculated as follows: Hours Sold ÷ Hours Worked.

The Hours Worked are carried forward into a period to match up with the Hours Sold, but then all of the valuable data about what has really happened in the workshop has been lost and the Manager is left with inaccurate information upon which to make strategic decisions. The practice of moving Hours Worked from one period to another is poor accounting practice and should not be undertaken in any circumstances because is completely distorts operational performance and the ability to reshape the business for future growth.

The monetary value of the Work In Progress is shown on the Balance Sheet and the biggest factor to affect the business is cash flow. If jobs are carried out and not invoiced, the jobs therefore cannot be converted into cash. It is for this reason that Work In Progress should be closely monitored and kept to an absolute minimum at all times.

Where Is The Technicians Salary Shown?
This is a question that is often asked and after discussing the Labour Cost of Sales, perhaps this is an appropriate juncture to explain things for the purpose of clarity.

It is a common misconception that the Labour Cost of Sales is equal to the Technicians total salary and the previous explanations have cleared up this misunderstanding. However, for simplicity, here's a straightforward list that will help to clear things up.

The Technicians salary is distributed across these six different accounting lines:

1) Labour Cost of Sales. The amount paid to the Technicians for the number of hours clocked onto jobs *(This will include Work In Progress, but will exclude the cost of Rectification and Idle Time)*.

2) Rectification. The amount paid to Technicians for time spent on Rectification for the purposes of rectifying faulty work. This is an expense rather than a cost of sale, which is covered later in the chapter.

3) Idle Time. The amount paid to Technicians for the time they are at the business, but are not clocked onto jobs. There are many reasons for Idle Time, which are covered later in the chapter.

4) Holiday. This is an expense and represents the amount paid to Technicians for the time they are on holiday. It cannot represent part of the Labour Cost of Sales because the Technicians are not available to work whilst on holiday.

5) Sickness. This is an expense and represents the amount paid to Technicians for the time they are on sick leave. It cannot represent part of the Labour Cost of Sales because the Technicians are not available to work whilst on sick leave.

6) Training. This is an expense and represents the amount paid to Technicians for the time they are on training. It cannot represent part of the Labour Cost of Sales because the Technicians are not available to work whilst training.

The proper allocation of the Technicians salary can sometimes appear to be over complicated and cumbersome to the uninitiated, but it's critical if the Service Department wishes to grow and develop its profitability. To function correctly, the Manager and the Accountant must exchange information effectively because a failure to provide the correct information to each other will produce incorrect analysis of the department. Incorrect analysis in business is like running at full speed in a forest with a blindfold over your eyes – even applying all your effort, you won't get very far and you'll end up bruised and battered by everything around you.

Getting the input correct for the Hours Worked and therefore the Labour Cost of Sales is of paramount importance in understanding and controlling the available resources within the Service Department.

Labour Gross Profit
The simple definition for this is Labour Sales minus Labour Cost of Sales, but given all of the inconsistencies that can appear in the Labour Cost of Sales, the following definition has much more clarity:

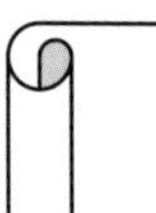

Labour Gross Profit
The invoice value of the Hours Sold
minus the amount paid to the
Technicians for the Hours Worked.

Magnum Motors Example:

A) Hours Bought = 160
B) Hours Attended = 140
C) Hours Worked = 126
D) Hours Sold = 150
E) Recovery Rate = £95
F) Wage Rate = £10
G) Other Expenses = £6,950

H) Labour Sales	=	£14,250	(D x E)
I) Labour Cost of Sales	=	£1,260	(C x F)
J) **Labour Gross Profit**	=	£12,990	(H – I)
K) Labour Gross Profit %	=	91.16%	(J ÷ H %)

The value of Labour Gross Profit (J) is affected most of all by the number of Hours Sold (D), or the volume of work that is undertaken. To a lesser degree it is also controlled by the price at which the work is sold to the customer (E) and the price paid to the Technicians for the Hours Worked (F).

It's important to note that the Labour Gross Profit % (K) is not affected by the number of Hours Sold because this is a key performance indicator that focuses only on the relationship between the buying price and the selling price of the Labour.

The Labour Gross Profit% is controlled at a Management level and is determined by the selling skills of the people who produce the invoices and present them to the customers thereby generating the Recovery Rate (E). The other controlling aspect is the average price paid to the Technicians for the Hours Worked (F), which is affected by prices paid for standard hourly rates, bonus payments and Overtime.

Although the value of Labour Gross Profit can vary greatly from month-to-month with seasonality, the Labour Gross Profit Percentage should not be altered by this fact. Therefore controlling the operational performance and profitability of the Service Department can be clearly separated into very distinct levels:

1) If the value of Labour Gross Profit is too low, more work is required.

2) If the Labour Gross Profit percentage is too low, either better selling skills are required at the point of invoicing to generate a higher Recovery Rate or the price being paid to the Technicians for the Hours Worked is too high, which may be a result of bonus payments or unnecessary Overtime.

It is very important that these two areas of operational performance are not confused or merged together because it is quite possible to suffer from low sales revenues and therefore a low Labour Gross Profit value, but still have a high Labour Gross Profit percentage.

A lack of understanding in these areas of performance often causes rash and ill-conceived business decisions to be made. For instance, if the value of Labour Gross Profit is too low and the Labour Gross Profit percentage is high, the remedy is to simply obtain more work; the remedy is not to increase the charge out rate. However, increasing prices in an attempt to elevate profitability is a route that is often taken by the naive Service Manager and it usually ends up with a significant reduction in customer retention.

It could be that the Service Department does not have enough work to fulfil its objectives and increasing prices may make the situation even worse. In some instances, it may be better to create a marketing campaign where prices are reduced in an attempt to gain more work and increase customer retention. However, it is imperative that the Management

Accounts are structured in a way that the effects of any such campaign are clearly visible, otherwise it's time to put the blindfold back over your eyes and run at full speed onto the forest in the vain hope that you might make it through to the other side.

The value of Labour Gross Profit and the Labour Gross Profit percentage are two completely different things and controlling them effectively relies upon the correct information being allocated to the Labour Cost of Sales.

Sub-Contract

This represents jobs that are undertaken by the company, but are carried out by a 3rd party. In other words, someone else will do the work. Typical examples here might be replacement windscreens, vehicle recovery, air conditioning, tyre fitment, paint and bodywork and other such tasks. It is common practice for all of the tasks to be collated for the whole period and simply shown as follows:

a) Sub Contract Sales = £12,160
b) Sub Contract Cost of Sales = £9,728
c) Sub Contract Gross Profit = £2,432 (a – b)
d) Sub Contract Gross Profit % = 20% (c ÷ a x 100)

The amount of Gross Profit here will vary greatly depending upon the type of work that is undertaken. For instance, some manufacturers state that all Sub Contract work undertaken for Warranty purposes is conducted at 0% mark up, whilst other manufacturers allow a mark up of 10% to be added. In other instances, the amount of Gross Profit available on a product or service may or may not be limited and perhaps one of the biggest factors to affect the profitability is the selling skills of the person who creates the invoice. In general terms, the Gross Profit % to aim for is around 20%, but as already stated, there are many limiting factors that will cause it to rise and fall each month. If the volume of Sub Contract work is consistently high, it may be worth investigating what work is being given away and whether it is possible for the company to invest in equipment to carry out this work in the future. Where this is considered, be sure to measure the investment against the possible Gross Profit to be generated to ensure a sufficient return on investment; there's no point in being a busy fool.

Lubricants and Oil

Within franchised dealerships where the Management Accounts are separated for Service and Parts departments, it's generally accepted that Lubricants and Oil sales are recorded within the Service Department, but in very rare cases the Accountant may decide to place them within the Parts Department, but which methodology is correct?

Argument #1

Oil is used by the Technicians, they obtain it themselves from a hose and they write it up on the job card therefore it should be included within the Service Department Accounts.

Argument #2

Oil is measured, monitored and ordered by the Parts Staff and Oil has a part number with which it is booked out to the customer therefore it should be included within the Parts Department Accounts.

Any of these two arguments could be used to justify where Lubricants and Oil sales are recorded and from the Lubricants and Oil point of view it really does not matter where it is recorded because the sales and profitability results will be the same. However, it should be noted that the sales and profits generated from Lubricants and Oil will make a significant contribution to the department in which it is located and it is this factor that requires serious thought about where it is placed. There is no right or wrong answer for where Lubricants and Oil sales are placed, but there is such a thing as common practice. Without question, by far the most common practice within the Motor Industry is for the Lubricants and Oils sales to be included within the Service Department and not the Parts Department.

Common practice is important in this instance because the placement of Lubricants and Oil sales will have a significant effect upon the departmental sales and profitability and when comparing one Service Department with another, the exclusion of Oil sales can create a sizable distortion; the same is true for the Parts Department of course.

The aim of this book to take the emotion out of these kinds of decisions in order to create a set of Management Accounts that are *consistent* across the Motor Industry and therefore become more useful to the Managers who use them to compare operational performance with other businesses. It is for this reason alone that arguments #1 and #2 do not enter into the discussion about which department oil sales are recorded because common practice overrules in this case. It is therefore recommended that where a company records Lubricants and Oils sales within the Parts Department, they should be relocated to the Service Department Accounts and the budget for each department is adjusted accordingly.

If this recommendation is ignored and Oil sales remain within the Parts Department, many of the key performance indicators will be incorrect and unusable for comparison with other businesses and Managers will be left at a disadvantage. It could be argued that Oil can be added or subtracted from statistics for comparison with other businesses, but that would just create more work and would also be admitting that the company is operating outside of common practice for which the reasoning must be questioned.

Lubricants and Oil sales are recorded simply with Sales, Cost of Sales and Gross Profit. The volumes of Oils sold are determined by the type and mix of work that is conducted and of course, the Technicians remembering to include the correct levels on the job card. However the Gross Profit % should remain relatively constant from month-to-month because the buying prices and the selling prices rarely change.

a) Oil Sales = £12,160
b) Oil Cost of Sales = £3,648
c) Oil Gross Profit = £8,512 (a – b)
d) Oil Gross Profit % = 70% (c ÷ a x 100)

The Gross Profit % can differ between businesses because the buying price can be altered significantly by the supplying oil company. In some cases, an oil company may provide a financial loan to the Service Department to assist with the purchase of new equipment and the loan is repaid to the oil company by purchasing oil at inflated prices, which increases the Oil Cost of Sales and decreases the Oil Gross Profit.

Tyres

The sale of Tyres comes under the same scrutiny as Lubricants and Oil in that it could be collated within the Service or the Parts Departments. Unfortunately, in this case there is no common practice to draw upon so the recommendation here is to follow the advice of the manufacturer where a franchise is held.

In order to capitalise upon the benefits of cash flow, many tyre suppliers offer imprest stock. This means that the Service Department does not have to purchase any tyres to hold in stock, the tyre company places them in stock, free of charge and asks for payment when they are sold.

Where imprest stock is available, the purchase price may be higher, but it is worth taking a lower profit margin for the benefits in cash flow because any profit that is made from the tyres has zero investment, in other words, it's profit for free.

Miscellaneous / Other Sales

These are terms that hopefully are only seen on the manufacturers Composite and not on the Management Accounts of a Service Department. This is because they represent sales of products or services that are not individually identified. These terms have a need to exist on a manufacturer's Composite because there needs to be a catch-all place for things that cannot be accounted for elsewhere. In other words, a dealer's

Management Accounts might contain an accounting line that the Manufacturer's Composite does not contain and this is the place where the activity it can be recorded.

The downside to having this accounting line present is that it can sometimes be used as a get-out-of-jail-free card and things can get dumped here to make things balance. This is of course poor accounting practice and great concern should be voiced if there are large values placed within these accounting lines because it is not possible to know what the activity relates to and that's bad news whichever way you choose to look at it.

Parts Sales

This is where there's a significant difference between a Service Department that is integrated within a franchised dealership and a stand-alone Service Centre.

The franchised dealership will not show Parts Sales within the Service Department Management Accounts. Any parts that are sold by the Service Department will be shown in the Management Accounts of the Parts Department.

The stand-alone Service Centre that is not part of a franchised dealership will show Parts Sales within the Service Centre Management Accounts, which will of course make overall profitability comparisons difficult between a franchised Service Department and a stand-alone Service Centre.

The Management Accounts for a stand-alone Service Centre usually show Parts sales on the four simple accounting lines.

Example:

a) Parts Sales	= £9,752	
b) Parts Cost of Sales	= £8,289	
c) Parts Gross Profit	= £1,463	(a – b)
d) Parts Gross Profit %	= 15.00%	(c ÷ a x 100)

Parts Sales
This captures the invoice value of all of the parts that have been sold and invoiced in the given accounting period. The volume and value of parts sold will vary depending upon the type and mix of work that is undertaken.

Parts Cost of Sales
This is simply the cost of the parts that have been sold in the same accounting period.

Parts Gross Profit
This is simply the invoice value of the parts sales minus the cost of those parts. The monetary value of the Gross Profit will change with the volume of parts that are sold and unlike other products that are sold, the Gross Profit percentage will also change because the buying margin on parts is not constant due to many overriding factors.

This again is another area of difference between a franchised dealership and a stand-alone Service Centre. Contrary to popular beliefs, the stand-alone Service Centre may receive higher levels of discount from a franchised Parts Department than the integrated franchised Service Department within the dealership. It is the subject that receives much debate and there are of course pro's and con's to each argument (another subject for a different book).

Manufacturers pricing policies are wide and varied with higher profit margins on fast moving items and lower margins on slow moving items. Parts taken from stock have higher profit margins to those parts which are ordered on a Vehicle Off Road (VOR) basis and some parts suppliers may give higher discounts than others. All of these factors, plus the type and mix of work that is undertaken have a large effect upon the Gross Profit percentage than is achieved with Parts Sales in the Service Centre. However, a reasonable level of Gross Profit percentage to expect on Parts Sales is upwards of 15%.

Departmental Gross Profit

This is a simple mathematical equation for accounting purposes and has no real operational significance. The Departmental Gross Profit is simply Total Sales minus total Cost of Sales. The Departmental Gross Profit percentage is also shown and is calculated as follows: Total Gross Profit ÷ Total Sales x 100.

From an operational perspective, the Departmental Gross Profit percentage has no real value to the Manager because the Gross Profit percentage is used to assess the performance of an individual product or service in its marketplace. Gross Profit percentage is worthless as an overall departmental figure because it averages out the profitability of all of the different products and services that have been sold. For instance, Labour Gross Profit may be 80%, Oil Sales may be at 60%, Sub Contract may be at 22%, Tyres may be at 12% and the combined average is... worthless.

This is because the Departmental Gross Profit percentage will change and trend up or down. The Manager will not know the reasons why by looking at this key performance indicator because all of the products and services have been merged together. This is why it is so important to begin reading Management Accounts from the top of the page and working down rather than from the bottom of the page and working up. When all of the products and services are merged together and then the balance of work and sales change, the departmental average will change but the Manager will be blind to any operational causes. In general terms, the Gross Profit percentage is asking the question, "How well is each individual product or service being exploited in its marketplace?" An averaged out Departmental Gross Profit percentage has no real value to the Manager.

Variable Expenses or Direct Expenses

This section contains a comprehensive listing of the expenses that are triggered by sales volume. They are not listed in any order of importance, some Management Accounts may even list them in alphabetical order with no preference or priority so there's no need for concern about the order of the layout, the only important factors are that they are separated from the Semi-Fixed or Indirect Expenses Let's take a closer look at some of the expenses that exist in this section.

Idle Time

This represents the amount of money paid to the Technicians for the time that is attended but not clocked onto jobs.

Magnum Motors example

A) Hours Bought	=	160	
B) Hours Attended	=	140	
C) Hours Worked	=	126	
D) Hours Sold	=	150	
E) Recovery Rate	=	£95	
F) Wage Rate	=	£10	
G) Other Expenses	=	£6,950	
H) Labour Sales	=	£14,250	(D x E)
I) Labour Cost of Sales	=	£1,260	(C x F)
J) Labour Gross Profit	=	£12,990	(H – I)
K) Labour Gross Profit %	=	91.16%	(J ÷ H %)
Expenses:			
L) **Idle Time**	=	£140	(B – C x F)

Idle Time is the remnant of Utilisation which is shown as a monetary value calculated by the number of hours that have been attended but not worked, multiplied by the Technicians hourly rate.

There are many reasons for the accumulation of Idle Time and numerous categories on dealer management systems to assist in the identification of these weak areas. Such categories might include moving vehicles, waiting for parts, cleaning, waiting for work and many other reasons. Whilst the Management Accounts may only show a single line to report the cost of Idle Time, it is critical that the Manager has a good grasp of how these expenses have been accumulated. Why are Technicians being paid to attend the business, but are not clocked onto jobs?

It's important to note that Idle Time does not represent "*unsold hours*" because hours are not available to sell, hours are only available to work. Hours Sold are controlled by the Service Reception or Invoicing Clerk and not the Technicians.

When Utilisation is increased by loading more jobs into the workshop, the Technicians will spend more time clocked onto jobs and the effect is that Idle Time will decrease and Hours Worked will increase by the same amount. This is because Hours Worked and Idle Time is simply a distribution of the Hours Attended.

Figure 1:

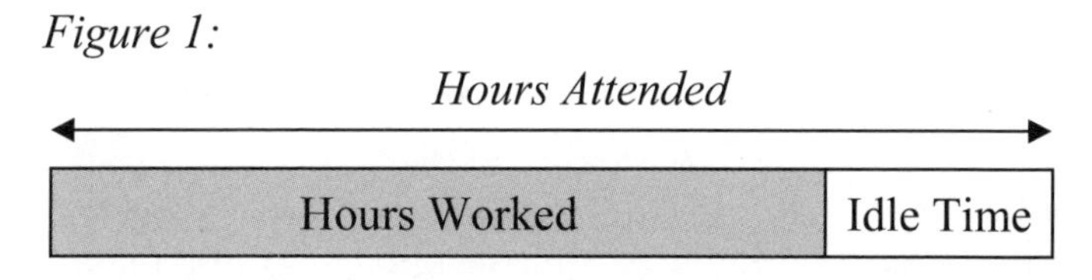

As the Hours Worked increase, Idle Time will decrease and vice versa. The objective is to keep the Technicians clocked onto jobs for as much of the Hours Attended as possible keeping the cost of Idle Time to a minimum. However, this result could be achieved by the Technicians taking a longer time to complete the same jobs, so take care to interpret the information correctly. A more detailed explanation of this phenomenon and the relationship between these important KPI can be found in *"The Law of the Service Department" (Chapter IV, Page 45 of How To Make More Profit With Your Service Department)*.

Idle Time is shown on the Management Accounts at the cost price of Labour and therefore may not appear to be a large amount of money. However, if additional work is loaded into the workshop and then sold to the customer, it can make a significant difference to the company profitability. For instance, let's say that an additional 10 hours of work is booked into the workshop and Idle Time is therefore reduced by 10 hours. Using the Magnum Motors figures, Idle Time would be reduced by £100 (10 hours @ £10). However, the Service Reception may sell 12 hours on the invoice and the additional revenue in Labour Sales would be £1,140 (12 hours Sold x £95). Idle Time may appear to be comparatively small amounts, but tapping into its potential can yield significant returns.

Consumables

This expense represents the cost of items that are used by Technicians on an ad hoc basis as they complete their work. Items here include nuts, bolts, washers, drills, releasing agent, seat covers, paper floor mats, steering wheel covers etc.

Some Service Departments might charge their customers for Consumables or Sundries and that will generate an additional accounting line within the Sales section along with Sub Contract and tyres etc.

Introductory Commission

This represents payments made to existing customers for referring new customers to the business. A recognised and well structured referral system pays high dividends in the future growth and stability of the company.

Sales Commission
This represents commissions paid to employees for selling items such as extended warranties and Service Plans etc.

This expense is to record commissions paid directly as a result of selling a product or a service, in other words the commission is triggered by the sale. For instance, sell one Service Plan, pay one commission payment. Sell two Service Plans, pay two commission payments and so on. This expense line does not include any target-related bonus payments because they are shown in the line called Bonus Payments.

Miscellaneous / Other Variable Expenses
Here again we have that accounting line that should not appear within departmental accounts, but will appear on a manufacturers Composite. These terms have a need to exist on a manufacturer's Composite because there needs to be a catch-all place for things that cannot be accounted for elsewhere.

* * * * *

Semi-Fixed Expenses or Indirect Expenses
This section contains a comprehensive listing of the expenses that are *not* triggered by sales volume. They are not listed in any order of importance, some Management Accounts may even list them in alphabetical order with no preference or priority so there's no need for concern about the layout. The important factors are that these expenses are separated from the Variable or Direct Expenses.

Salaries & Wages
This represents the basic salaries paid to the personnel of the Service Department who are not Technicians. *(The Technicians salaries are recorded elsewhere.)*

Typically, this may include the salaries of the Service Manager, Service Receptionist, Invoicing Clerk, Warranty Clerk, Foreman, Drivers, Cleaners, Vehicle Jockey, Clerical staff and any part of a Technical Experts salary that is not included within the Hours Attended.

Target-related bonus payments made to employees are not included here.

NI & Pension
In countries where National Insurance (NI) and pension payments are made for employees, these expenses are usually shown separately to the basic salaries and sales commissions so that a fair and realistic comparison on salaries can be made.

Holiday
This expense records the salary paid to Technicians whilst they are on holiday. It cannot represent part of the Labour Cost of Sales because the Technicians are not available to work whilst on Holiday.

Sickness
This expense records the salary paid to Technicians whilst they are on sick leave. It cannot represent part of the Labour Cost of Sales because the Technicians are not available to work whilst on sick leave. This is separated from other expenses so that any problems with absenteeism can be quickly identified.

Training Cost Salaries
This expense represents the amount of money paid to Technicians for any training that is conducted either on site at the company or off site at a training centre or college. It cannot represent part of the Labour Cost of Sales because the Technicians are not available to work whilst they are engaged in training.

An apportionment of the Apprentices salaries is also included within this expense. There are no hard and fast rules for apportionment here, but the most popular method in use is as follows:

Apprentice in year 1:
100% of the salary is included here because all of their time is spent with other Technicians and is classed as training.

Apprentice in year 2:
50% of the salary is included here and the other 50% is included within the Hours Attended because there is an expectation that an Apprentice in their second year will be producing work for 50% of the time that they are in attendance and therefore 50% is classed as training.

Apprentice in year 3:
25% of the salary is included here and the other 75% is included within the Hours Attended because there is an expectation that an Apprentice in their third year will be producing work for 75% of the time that they are in attendance and therefore the remaining 25% is classed as training.

Training Course Costs
This expense records the cost of the training itself as opposed to any salaries that are paid to Technicians whilst attending training.

This expense captures the cost of all training for all Service Department personnel, technical or non-technical and will include training course fees, accommodation, travel and subsistence.

Subscriptions
This represents fees and subscriptions payable to industry journals, magazines, governing bodies, and trade bodies.

Bonus Payments
This relates to any target-related bonus payments that have been made to Service Department personnel. For instance, if the Service Manager is paid a bonus based on achieving a certain profit objective for the department, this bonus payment will be included here.

Please note any bonus payments made to Technicians are not included within this expense line. Bonus payments paid to Technicians should be included within the Labour Cost of Sales because those bonus payments are a reward for some form of production and therefore they should increase the cost of the Hours Worked.

Rectification
This expense is sometimes known as Goodwill, Policy Cost or Policy Adjustment. This is where a Technician has worked on a job, but the customer has returned with a problem. The Technician will need to

clock onto this job with a new job card to rectify the problem, but the customer will not be charged again.

The monetary value represents the amount paid to the Technicians for the amount of time clocked onto Rectification work. For example, if a Technician is paid £10 per hour and Rectification equates to 4 hours, the value recorded in this expense will be £40.

This is an expense that needs to be closely monitored in line with the company's right-first-time objectives because if this expense is showing an increasing trend it could be that Technicians are working quickly, but taking short-cuts and compromising the task in hand.

Another indicator here is that an increasing trend could be a sign of weak Service Management, a person who cannot say "no" to non-genuine complaints. Compare the trend of this expense with any Customer Satisfaction Programmes that may be running.

Having customer complaints is not a bad thing, it's how those complaints are dealt with that decides customer satisfaction and customer retention.

Computer Costs

This represents the money payable to computer maintenance contracts and equipment costs that are specific to the Service Department. It may also include the cost of bespoke software agreements and franchise operating systems, DMS charges, subscriptions, maintenance agreements, but it does not include the development cost of web sites because that ought to be shown as a marketing expense.

Maintenance / Equipment Costs
This represents all of the costs associated with the maintenance and repair of special tools and equipment within the Service Department. This will include the cost of maintaining ramps, rolling roads and heating equipment etc.

Depreciation of Equipment
This represents the amount of money that Service Department equipment has been depreciated.

Depreciation reduces the current value of the equipment and in doing so reduces the profitability of the department. The company therefore has a lower taxation liability. The amount of depreciation is usually decided by the Accountant, but this area is governed by Taxation Law and there are maximum limits that equipment can be depreciated by within a 12-month period. Taxation Law relating to depreciation changes frequently and will be different for each country.

Warranty Write off
Where a business holds a franchise, Warranty work is undertaken by the dealer on behalf of the franchise and payment is made providing that certain criteria are followed. In the event where the criteria are not followed or an invalid Warranty claim has been made, the franchise will refuse to pay for the Warranty work undertaken. In this case, the dealer will not receive payment and will therefore have to write off the declared profit and this is the expense line where the value of the Warranty write off is shown.

Vehicle cleaning
This represents the cost of cleaning customers' vehicles after any service or repair work has been conducted. This should include the cost of all cleaning materials.

Vehicle Running Costs
This represents the total operating costs and charges associated with the running of the vehicles that are in use by the Service Department, excluding Courtesy Vehicles. Items here will include fuel, PDI charges, road fund licenses, tyres, accident repairs, scratch removal and servicing etc. Vehicle insurance is not shown here, it's shown within the company Overheads.

Vehicle Funding
This is the cost of the borrowings incurred for Service Department vehicles. This does not include the cost of funding Courtesy Vehicles.

Vehicle Depreciation
There is no hard a fast ruling as to how depreciation should be applied, but some manufacturers do provide guidelines. In general terms, some Accountants apply depreciation at a flat rate of between 2% and 5% per month, whilst other may apply a monetary sum per vehicle each month. Of course these percentages and monetary figures are for example only, the true cost of depreciation is wholly dependent upon the specific vehicles and the franchise held.

Courtesy Vehicle Running Costs
This represents the total operating costs and charges associated with the running of the courtesy vehicles

that are in use by the Service Department. Items here will include fuel, PDI charges, road fund licenses, tyres, accident repairs, scratch removal and servicing etc. Vehicle insurance is not shown here, it's shown within the company Overheads.

Courtesy Vehicle Funding
This is the cost of the borrowings incurred for all Courtesy vehicles.

Courtesy Vehicle Depreciation
This is the monthly cost of depreciation applied to the Courtesy vehicles.

Credit Card Charges
When customers pay for their work using a credit card, the company will be charged a commission by the credit card company, which is around 2% of the transaction.

Taking funds on credit cards is not usually a high value transaction, but there can be many transactions so credit card charges can be rather high. Some companies charge the customer an additional 2% for payment by credit card, but this fact must be advertised in the building somewhere and it's a policy that may not contribute well towards Customer Satisfaction.

Advertising
This represents the total expenditure for the advertising and promotion of the Service Department, which includes direct mail, Internet campaigns and telephone marketing initiatives. Where a franchise is held, any support that is provided by the franchise

should be shown here to show the true financial expenditure of the department.

General Expenses
This is the line to account for things that cannot be placed elsewhere and it should therefore contain very small values because the Manager will not know what these expenses relate to. However, it will appear on a manufacturer's Composite because it performs a catch-all facility for the document because dealers Management Accounts are not all the same.

Total Departmental Expenses
Here there can be a big difference between a Service Department that is integrated within a franchised dealership and a stand-alone Service Centre.

Firstly, in the case of the franchised Service Department, the total departmental expenses represent the sum total of all of the "*operational*" expenses for the Service Department and do not contain any of the company Overheads.

In the case of a stand-alone Service Centre, some Accountants show the operational expenses, but also include the cost of the total business Overheads, which significantly distorts the operational analysis of the Service Centre. This is considered to be poor accounting practice.

Recommendation For Structural Change
In the case of the stand-alone business, it is recommended that the operational side of the Service Centre activities are accounted for as a department

and the Overheads are separated from operational activities and shown accordingly.

There is a very strong and compelling reason for this recommendation and it's because a Service Centre Manager who is responsible for improving operation performance in the workshop does not have any direct control over the Overheads of the company. This can have a negative effect upon the motivation of the Manager because the cost of Overheads can rise outside of the Manager's control and the performance of the workshop will be seen to diminish, where in fact, this may not be the case at all.

In these cases, it is not uncommon to see Managers give up on cost control and operational performance improvement because they feel that there is nothing they can do about it. Therefore simply making this structural change so that the accounting structure shows the workshop as a department that is all within the control of the Manager can have a massive effect upon the mindset of the Manager and therefore operational performance. Business costs that are outside of the control of the Service Centre Manager such as Rent, Rates and Professional Fees etcetera, should be shown separately within the company Overheads.

If company Overheads are not separated from the operational side of the business, expenses will be reported as a total figure and usually expressed as a percentage of Turnover.

Let's say that a business is reporting total Expenses as 47% of Turnover and this figure is higher than would be liked. What exactly would this figure mean and how would anyone go about reducing it? The problem is that the "causes" of the expenses are not separated and merging them in this way fuses together three totally different types of expenses:

1) Departmental expenses triggered by volume
2) Departmental expenses not triggered by volume
3) Company Overheads

Which one is too high; is it all of them or just one of them?

Is the department under control and the business Overheads too high or is it the other way around?

When operational expenses are merged with company expenses and reported as a single figure, the information is rendered worthless because the Manager is blind to what is happening and therefore cannot ascertain any influence.

In the case of the Service Department that is integrated within a franchise dealership, the total departmental expenses represent the sum total of all of the expenses for the whole of the Service Department, which may also be expressed as a percentage of Turnover with the following calculation: Expenses ÷ Turnover x 100.

The problem here of course is that there is still a merging of operational information which leaves the Manager blind to what is happening at an operational level.

Operationally speaking, reporting a total expenses figure and producing an average is pretty worthless because the Manager will not be able to clearly see the effects of any actions that are implemented. By all means, keep an eye on this figure but pay far more attention to each expense category individually.

Maternity and Paternity Leave
Although not usually listed in Management Accounts or Composite, consideration should also be given to this important area. It should not be classified as Holiday pay or Sick pay.

Direct Profit
This is also known as Departmental Profit, Operating Profit or more colloquially, the bottom line. This is a simple mathematical equation, which is calculated by taking the total Departmental Gross Profit, plus any bonus where applicable, minus all Departmental Expenses. Operationally speaking, it is of course an "effect" rather than a "cause" therefore it can only be influenced by other operational factors.

As stated in Chapter IV, it's pointless beginning the analysis of the department here because there's so much information that goes into it. Proper analysis of the department examines this figure last of all because it is the understanding of the individual components that make up this figure that unleashes the real power of performance improvement.

Many Management Accounts will illustrate this figure as a percentage of Turnover, but it is always the trend of this Key Performance Indicator that is of primary importance.

Magnum Motors Example:

A) Hours Bought	=	160	
B) Hours Attended	=	140	
C) Hours Worked	=	126	
D) Hours Sold	=	150	
E) Recovery Rate	=	£95	
F) Wage Rate	=	£10	
G) Other Expenses	=	£6,950	
H) Labour Sales	=	£14,250	(D x E)
I) Labour Cost of Sales	=	£1,260	(C x F)
J) Labour Gross Profit	=	£12,990	(H – I)
K) Labour Gross Profit %	=	91.16%	(J ÷ H %)
Expenses:			
L) Idle Time	=	£140	(B – C x F)
M) Holiday, Sickness Etc	=	£200	(A – B x F)
N) Other Expenses	=	£6,950	
O) Total Expenses	=	£7,290	(L + M + N)
P) **Department Profit**	**=**	**£5,700**	(J – O)
Q) **Department Profit %**	**=**	**40.00%**	(P ÷ H %)

Knowing how to calculate the Direct Profit percentage is one thing, but knowing how to influence the trend is what is really required and that information is gleaned from the true understanding of both financial and commercial awareness.

The key to success with improving operational performance in the Service Department is to understand the relationships between Utilisation, Productivity and Overall Efficiency and have the ability to accurately forecast how these key performance indicators will change before new initiatives are implemented. Failure to understand these factors in advance of implementing new actions is nothing more that strategic guesswork. Taking the guesswork out of business improvement means that people have to *make* change happen, rather than to *let* change happen. It's often tough, challenging and requires the determination to succeed. The act of *making* change happen is strictly reserved for top achievers.

"The only people who have the ability to change and seek improvements are those who want to, and not everyone wants to."

- Jeff Smith

CHAPTER IX

UNDERSTANDING THE PARTS DEPARTMENT

"Drive thy business,
or it will drive thee"

- Benjamin Franklin

CHAPTER IX

UNDERSTANDING THE PARTS DEPARTMENT

Of all of the departmental Management Accounts structures, the Parts Department is without question the most simplistic and easiest to understand. Just like the Sales Department, this is a product-based accounting structure without the complexities of buying and selling time.

In simplistic terms, the Parts Department is all about buying and selling Parts and of course, generating a profit from those sales. The skill lies in the Manager's ability to forecast what Parts will be required in advance and keeping those parts in stock. However, if Parts are ordered for stock and remain unsold, the cost to the business is colossal because it soaks up working capital and the business could run out of cash. Maintaining the balance between making a profit and managing cash flow is of paramount importance.

There are numerous factors that affect the operational performance of the Parts Department; some are external issues such as improvements in technology, the frequency of supply and customer loyalty. Some issues are of an internal nature such as interdepartmental policies, relationships and customer discount structures. All of these factors have a direct impact upon profitability and the secret to success lies in the Manager's speed of reaction to change.

Parts Sales

This is the monetary value of the Parts that have been sold and invoiced in a given period of time and it is the value after discount has been given and does not include taxation. Note that this is not the retail price of the Parts.

Typically, total Parts will not be shown as a single entry, they will be categorised to show activity within each income stream. These accounting lines will be different for a Parts Department that is an integrated part of a franchised dealership and an independent parts factor business. This is because a franchised dealership will have integrated Service Department and/or Bodyshop where Parts Sales are not recorded within those departments; they are recorded here within the integrated Parts Department. Here are some examples of how Parts Sales are categorised, but some manufacturer's Composites go even further and show separation between franchise and non-franchise parts sales.

Retail Sales – This represents the invoice value of Parts and accessories sold over the counter or through an accessories or merchandising store to retail customers.

Trade - This represents the invoice value of Parts sold to other businesses who are in the same trade. These may be sold on site or delivered by the company Parts Vehicles. For instance, independent Service Centres, Bodyshops or other main dealers holding different franchises. Note that this does not include sales to other dealers who hold the same franchise.

Inter-Dealer – Sales of Parts to other dealers and authorised repairers, outside of your own business, who hold the same franchise.

Secondary Network – Sales of Parts to Retail Status dealers, owned by someone else, but hold the same franchise. *(Not all franchises have a secondary network i.e. Approved Service Centres or Approved Bodyshops).*

Note that this section does not include transactions in a business or dealer group where a hub and satellites are in operation.

Parts movements between a hub and satellite should not be recorded as Parts Sales but rather as a stock transfer. The business who sells and invoices the Parts should record the Parts Sales within their Management Accounts.

Service Retail – Where a franchised dealership has an integrated Service Department, this section includes the invoice value of Parts Sales on customers vehicles who are classified as Retail Customers within the Service Department.

Service Internal – Invoice value of Parts sold to the workshop for all work carried out on vehicles for the integrated Sales Department. This will include new vehicles, used vehicles and demonstrators etc.

Service Warranty – Invoice value of Parts sold to the workshop, which are to be reclaimed on the franchise warranty system

Bodyshop Retail - Where a franchised dealership has an integrated Bodyshop, this section includes the invoice value of Parts Sales on customers vehicles who are classified as Retail Customers within the Bodyshop.

Bodyshop Insurance – Invoice value of parts fitted to vehicles that have been authorised by Insurance companies.

Bodyshop Internal – Invoice value of Parts sold to the Bodyshop for all work carried out on vehicles for the integrated Sales Department. This will include new vehicles, used vehicles and demonstrators etc.

Bodyshop Warranty – Invoice value of Parts sold to the Bodyshop, which are to be reclaimed on the franchise warranty system

Other Sales – Invoice value of any other items that have been sold by the Parts Department that have not been categorised separately.

Total Parts Sales – This is the sum total of all Parts Sales categories listed and represents the total Parts Turnover for the period at invoice value.

Parts Cost Of Sales (COS)
This represents the purchase price of the Parts that have been sold. Each category listed for Parts Sales will also be listed for Parts Cost of Sales

Parts Gross Profit
This is a simple mathematical equation that takes the Sales or Turnover and deducts the Cost of Sales. Each

category listed for Parts Sales and Parts Cost of Sales will also be listed for Gross Profit. This will also be expressed as a percentage for each income stream showing how well each category performs within its marketplace.

The difference in Gross Profit % between each of these categories can be significant and it's important to understand why these differences exist so that control can be ascertained. The following example is simplified for illustration purposes only:

Figure 1: Understanding Gross Profit

	Sales	COS	GP	GP%
Retail	2,376	1,592	784	33%
Trade	19,560	16,235	3,325	17%
Service	24,710	18,532	6,178	25%
Other	875	507	368	42%
Total	**47,521**	**36,866**	**10,655**	**22.42%**

Just look at the huge variances in the Gross Profit % column. Overall, the Departmental Gross Profit is 22.42%, but because it is an average of the whole department, it reveals absolutely nothing in terms of operational performance. All of the income streams must be visible to the Manager if any sense is to be made of the interpretation.

Gross Profit is an individual income stream measure and not an average departmental measure. It exists so that the Manager can assess where the strengths and weaknesses are within the department and to take the appropriate actions.

A good set of Management Accounts for the Parts Department will list all of the different income streams separately showing the Sales, Cost of Sales, Gross Profit and Gross Profit % for each sector. This might mean that there are many different accounting lines, which is the reason why a set of Management Accounts can first appear to be large and complicated. However, although there may be many accounting lines, they are only reporting the first three steps of the five basic accounting steps that you need to know.

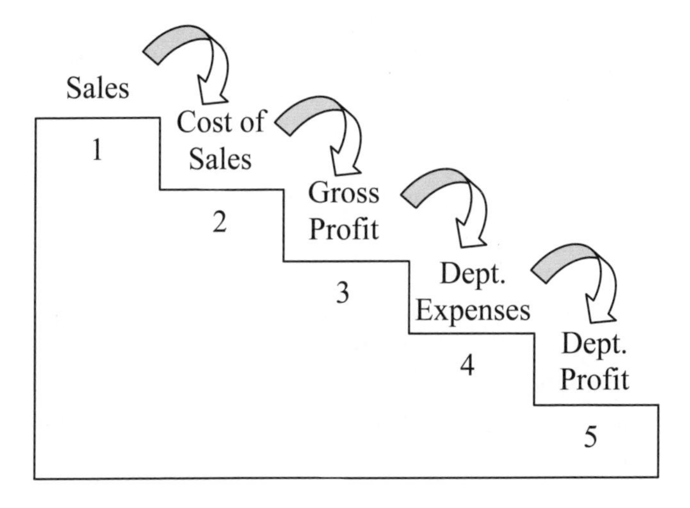

The fact that there is more information on each of the first three steps does not make the Management Accounts more complicated, in fact the reverse is true. The more separation of information there is on each step, the easier it is to interpret and understand what is happening at an operational level.

Departmental Gross Profit is not much use at all, unless it is known how it has been achieved and that requires clear and concise separation.

Bonus & Incentives

This represents any bonus payments or incentives received from parts suppliers or manufacturers. These are usually incentive payments made to the company for the achievement of a parts purchasing target.

These bonus payments should not be shown within the Parts Cost of Sales because that would have the effect of reducing the value and therefore showing a higher Gross Profit and Gross Profit %.

In terms of interpretation, this could mislead Managers to believe that they are buying and selling Parts with better margins than they really are – you can't make a good decision with bad information.

Achieving Parts purchasing targets is certainly not guaranteed and therefore Bonus payments may be achieved and payable in one accounting period, but not in another. If Bonus payments are included prior to the calculation of Parts Gross Profit, the Gross Profit % will be influenced by target achievement, it will be reporting very erratically and it will be wholly inaccurate.

Gross Profit is a measure that exists to ascertain the control over buying prices and selling prices. The achievement of parts purchasing targets is a different operational measure altogether and therefore any bonus and incentive payments received for the achievement of a purchasing target should be should be accounted for separately and totally excluded from any Gross Profit calculations.

Parts Department Expenses

Departmental Expenses fall into two categories; those triggered by sales volume and those not triggered by sales volume. Just as a reminder *Variable* or *Direct* are triggered by sales volume and *Semi-Fixed* or *Indirect* are not triggered by sales volume. However, there are no *Variable* or *Direct* expenses within the Parts Department, they are all *Semi-Fixed* or *Indirect,* which makes life much easier.

This section contains a comprehensive listing of the expenses that can be found within the Parts Department. They are not listed in any order of importance or preference so there's no need for concern about the order or layout.

Salaries and Wages

This is the amount paid in basic wages, salaries and bonuses to all Parts Department personnel. It usually includes the company's statutory and voluntary contributions such as sick pay, holiday pay, health care insurance etc.

Note, some companies include Taxation and pensions where applicable, where other companies might have a separate accounting line.

NI & Pensions

Where applicable, this is to capture the amount paid in National Insurance and Pension Contributions.

Training

This represents the cost of training for the whole department which includes the cost of the attendance, overnight accommodation, travel and subsistence.

Vehicle Running Expenses

This is the total charge for the running of all vehicles in use by the Parts Department with the exception of the Parts delivery vehicles. Expenses here will include fuel, PDI charges, road fund licenses, tyres, accident repairs, scratch removal and servicing. Vehicle insurance is not shown here, that is shown within the company Overheads.

Vehicle Funding

This is the cost of the borrowings incurred for Parts Department vehicles. This does not include the cost of funding delivery vehicles.

Vehicle Depreciation

There is no hard and fast ruling on how depreciation should be applied, but some manufacturers do provide guidelines.

In general terms, some Accountants might apply depreciation at a flat rate of between 2% and 5% per month, whilst other may apply a monetary sum per vehicle each month. Of course these percentages and monetary figures are for example only, the true cost of depreciation is wholly dependent upon the specific vehicles and the franchise held.

Parts Delivery Vehicle Running Costs

This represents the total operating costs and charges associated with the running of the delivery vehicles that are in use by the Parts Department. Items here will include fuel, PDI charges, road fund licenses, tyres, accident repairs, scratch removal and servicing etc. Vehicle insurance is not shown here, that is shown within the company Overheads.

Parts Delivery Vehicle Funding
This is the cost of the borrowings incurred for all Parts Delivery vehicles.

Parts Delivery Vehicle Depreciation
This is the monthly cost of depreciation applied to the Parts Delivery vehicles.

Note: The cost of Parts Vehicles and Parts Delivery Vehicles are separated so that the Manager can conduct a proper evaluation of the Parts Delivery service that is offered. Armed with this separation of information, it is possible to calculate the value of Parts that need to be sold and delivered in order for a Parts Delivery Vehicle to reach a point of financial breakeven. The information is critical when justifying if an additional Parts Delivery vehicle is viable or indeed if the Parts Delivery service is viable in the first instance. After all, there's no point in running delivery vehicles at a loss, is there?

Computer Costs
This represents the money payable to computer maintenance contracts and equipment costs that are specific to the Parts Department. It may also include the cost of bespoke software agreements, price updates, franchise operating systems, DMS charges, license fees, subscriptions, maintenance agreements, but it does not include the development cost of web sites because that ought to be shown as a marketing expense.

Maintenance / Equipment Costs
This represents all of the costs associated with the maintenance and repair of plant and equipment used

within the Parts Department. This will include the cost of maintaining racking and bin systems.

Depreciation of Equipment
This represents the amount of money that Parts Department equipment has been depreciated.

Depreciation reduces the current value of the equipment and in doing so reduces the profitability of the department. The company therefore has a lower taxation liability. The amount of depreciation is usually decided by the Accountant, but this area is governed by Taxation Law and there are maximum limits that equipment can be depreciated within a 12 month period. Taxation Law relating to depreciation changes frequently and will be different for each country.

Introductory Commission
This represents payments made to existing customers for referring new customers to the business. A recognised and well structured referral system pays high dividends in the future growth and stability of the company.

Credit Card Charges
When customers pay for their Parts using a credit card, the company will be charged a commission by the credit card company, which is around 2% of the transaction.

Taking funds on credit cards is not usually a high value transaction, but there can be many transactions so credit card charges can be rather high. Some companies charge the customer an additional 2% for payment by credit card, but this fact must be advertised in the building somewhere and it's a policy that may not contribute well towards Customer Satisfaction.

Advertising
This represents the total expenditure for the advertising and promotion of the Parts Department, which includes direct mail, Internet campaigns and telephone marketing initiatives. Where a franchise is held, any support that is provided by the franchise should be shown here to show the true financial expenditure of the department.

Stock Transfers
Where a franchised dealer operates a Hub and Satellite system, this expense captures the cost of handling and delivery charges incurred for the transfer of parts stock between branches.

Warranty Write Off/ Warranty Adjustment
Where a business holds a franchise, Warranty work is undertaken by the dealer on behalf of the franchise and payment is made providing that certain criteria are followed. In the event where the criteria are not followed or an invalid Warranty claim has been made, the franchise will refuse to pay for the Warranty work undertaken.

In this case, the dealer will not receive payment and will therefore have to write off the declared profit and this is the expense line where the value of the Warranty write off is shown.

Subscriptions

This represents fees and subscriptions payable to industry journals, magazines, governing bodies, and trade bodies.

Obsolete Provision

Unlike food goods, Parts do not have a "sell by" printed on them, but from a commercial point of view, there is a limited amount of time for them to remain is stock because new vehicles are being launched and demand for older parts diminishes. Once this time has expired, those old parts are said to be past their sell by date, or in other words, they become obsolete.

This expense is a provision made for obsolete stock, which is used to write off parts stock, usually at the financial year end. There are numerous methods for calculating this provision ranging from a percentage of the departmental Gross Profit to applying an age limit.

Some companies state that when parts have been in stock for 1 year, 50% of their value is written off. When parts reach the ripe old age of 2 years in stock, the remaining balance of their value is written off. In this case, there should not be any parts left in stock that have been on the shelf for a period of more than 2 years. Some companies apply a rather more strict approach to this provision and apply the 50% rule after six months and the remaining value after 12 months. In this case, there should not be any parts left in stock that have been on the shelf for a period of more than 1 year.

The idea behind this provision is to provide a monthly value to the Management Accounts that will be equal to the value of Parts that become obsolete. Regardless the methodology used to calculate the value for the provision, as a guideline, the provision should not be more than 1% of the Parts stock value each month.

Example:

A) Stock Value £315,210
B) Monthly Provision £3,000
C) Obsolete Provision 0.95%

If the calculation for the provision is greater than 1% of the stock value, this could mean that Parts Stock is too high, Parts are not being sold quickly enough and therefore becoming obsolete. One key performance indicator to track and trend to maintain the right balance between stock value and obsolete provision is True Stock Turn.

This obsolete provision is made on a monthly basis to even out the expense rather than having one big hit at the financial year end. In addition to this, it's better to account for this on a monthly basis because not all companies have the same financial year end so the monthly provision eliminates comparison distortions.

Stock Adjustments

This expense represents any stock losses, differences between stock-take values and book stock values or any write down values that are not covered by the obsolete provision.

General/Miscellaneous Expenses
This is the line to account for things that cannot be placed elsewhere and it should therefore contain very small values because the Manager will not know what these expenses relate to. However, it will appear on a manufacturer's Composite because it performs a catch-all facility for the document because dealers Management Accounts are not all the same. Unfortunately it must exist, but keep a close eye on what goes into this line.

Total Departmental Expenses
Here there can be a big difference between a Parts Department that is integrated within a franchised dealership and a stand-alone Parts Factor.

Firstly, in the case of the franchised Parts Department, the total departmental expenses represent the sum total of all of the "*operational*" expenses for the Parts Department and do not contain any of the company Overheads.

In the case of a stand-alone Parts Factor, some Accountants show the operational expenses, but also include the cost of the total business Overheads, which significantly distorts the operational analysis of the department. This is considered to be poor accounting practice.

Recommendation For Structural Change
In the case of the stand-alone business, it is recommended that the operational side of the Parts Factor activities are accounted for as a department and the Overheads are separated from operational activities and shown accordingly.

There is a very strong and compelling reason for this recommendation and it's because a Parts Factor Manager who is responsible for improving operation performance does not have any direct control over the Overheads of the company. This can have a negative effect upon motivation of the Manager because the cost of Overheads can rise outside of the Manager's control and the performance of the Parts will be seen to diminish, where in fact, this may not be the case at all.

In these instances, it is not uncommon to see Managers give up on cost control and operational performance improvement because they feel that there is nothing they can do about it. Therefore simply making this structural change so that the accounting structure shows the Parts operation as a department that is all within the control of the Manager can have a massive effect upon the mindset of the Manager and therefore operation performance. Business costs that are outside of the control of the Parts Manager such as Rent, Rates and Professional Fees etcetera, should be shown separately within the company Overheads.

If company Overheads are not separated from the operational side of the business, expenses will be reported as a total figure and usually expressed as a percentage of Turnover.

When operational expenses are merged with company expenses and reported as a single figure, the information is rendered worthless because the Manager is blind to what is happening and therefore cannot ascertain any influence.

In the case of the Parts Department that is integrated within a franchised dealership, the total departmental expenses represent the sum total of all of the expenses for the whole of the Parts Department, which may be expressed as a percentage of Turnover with the following calculation: Expenses ÷ Turnover x 100. As a general guideline, the total value of expenses within the Parts Department should be less than 8% of the departmental turnover.

Direct Profit

This is also known as Departmental Profit, Operating Profit or more colloquially, the bottom line. This is a simple mathematical equation, which is calculated by taking the total Departmental Gross Profit, plus any bonus where applicable, minus all Departmental Expenses. Operationally speaking, it is of course an "effect" rather than a "cause" therefore it can only be influenced by other operational factors within the department.

As stated in Chapter IV, it's pointless beginning the analysis of the department here because there's so much information that goes into it. Proper analysis of the department examines this figure last of all because it is the understanding of the individual components that make up this figure that unleashes the real power of performance improvement.

Many Management Accounts will illustrate this figure as a percentage of Turnover, but it is always the trend of this Key Performance Indicator that is of primary importance. As a guideline, the Direct Profit percentage should be greater than 12% of Turnover within the Parts Department, but this of course is influenced by many different factors. Knowing how to calculate the Direct Profit percentage is one thing, but knowing how to influence the trend is what is really required and that information is gleaned from the true understanding of both financial and commercial awareness.

The key to success with improving operational performance in the Parts Department is to understand the relationships between Direct Profit, Circulation of Investment, True Stock Turn, Return on Investment and have the ability to accurately forecast how these key performance indicators will change before new initiatives are implemented.

At the heart of every highly profitable Parts operation there will be a Manager who is controlling how Parts are being purchased and balancing parts purchases with Stock Turn. Coupled with this, they will be balancing Trade Sales activity with Parts Vehicle breakeven volumes. It's all too easy to fall into the trap of chasing other people's targets.

"Drive thy business,
or it will drive thee"

- Benjamin Franklin

Chapter IX

Understanding The Bodyshop

"The only place where success comes before work, is in the dictionary"."

- Vidal Sasson

CHAPTER IX

UNDERSTANDING THE BODYSHOP

The primary function of a Bodyshop is to buy and sell time as opposed to buying and selling tangible products which are the main activities of Sales and Parts Departments. Before reading this chapter, please read Chapter VI because the differences in the accounting structures for buying and selling products and services are explained in detail throughout.

The financial structure of the Management Accounts for the Bodyshop is very much the same as the financial structure for the Service Department, but this does not mean that the operational functionality is the same, in fact, they are very different. Before going head first into the Bodyshop, let's review some of the similarities and differences that exist.

Bodyshop Versus Service Department
This section is particularly helpful to a franchised dealership that has both a Bodyshop and a Service Department because it covers the most important similarities and differences between them.

Financially speaking, the Bodyshop and Service Department are the same in that they both have Labour Sales and they both have people with technical skills working on jobs, but that is where the similarities end. Commercially, there's a huge difference in the way that the two businesses operate.

When a job goes into the Service Department, invariably, it is worked upon by one person and in most cases the job is completed within the same day. However, when a job goes into the Bodyshop it may be worked upon by at least three different people and in three different departments; Fitters, Panel Beaters and Painters and the job usually takes much longer than one day to complete.

Although the reporting of information is the same for both departments, it is important to understand that the operational performance is completely different because of the different ways in which the jobs are handled.

Both departments measure key performance indicators such as Utilisation, Productivity and Overall Efficiency and the mathematics for these key performance indicators are identical, but the interpretation of the information is different.

In many cases the actions that need to be taken in order to improve performance are the same for both departments, *but*, and it is a very big *but*...although the ideas for improvement are the same the implementation of those ideas into the workplace is completely different because the jobs are handled in different ways.

For instance, within a Service Department, Utilisation may be calculated for the whole department, whereas in a Bodyshop it may be more beneficial to measure the Utilisation of the Fitters, Panel Beaters and Painters separately because they all work with vehicles with different methodology.

Why Measure Separately In The Bodyshop?
Over the past 20 years, technology in vehicle production has increased significantly and model ranges receive face-lifts more frequently in the manufacturers' pursuit of increasing or stabilising market share. Both of these factors mean that vehicles are now more complex and more diverse in their construction and the impact upon the Fitters is that some jobs may take longer to complete as they are constantly learning how new vehicles are constructed.

However, this advance in technology has had little effect upon the Panel Beater, but this role will be affected by the use of so called "Green Parts". This is where a used panel may be fitted as opposed to a new panel or where the cost of repairing the damaged panel is greater than the cost of fitting a used panel. Only time will tell in this area.

Further advances in technology have come from the paint manufacturers. Colour matching systems are now far more accurate than ever before, the paints are easier to apply and the paint and lacquer drying times have been reduced considerably, which means that jobs can be painted more quickly and with less rectification.

All of these factors affect the flow and speed of completion of the jobs in the Bodyshop and that is why it is wise to measure the operational performance of each area separately. When improvements are implemented in one area, those improvements may not carry over to another area. For instance, if new technology means that paint and lacquer drying times are reduced and therefore vehicles can be painted faster, that gain in operational performance does not mean that the Panel Beater or the Fitter will be able to work any faster. An improvement of this nature could simply mean that the Painter will run out of work and that's the main reason why it's very important to measure these three areas separately.

All of that being said, the main areas of discussion between a Bodyshop and a Service Department lies within the Labour Gross Profit %.

LABOUR GROSS PROFIT

Over the past few years, Labour Rates within Service Departments have increased substantially and at the time of writing, the average Labour Rate can be anywhere from £65 per hour or more in the UK. During this time the Bodyshop Labour Rates have been restricted by the working practices of the Insurance Companies which means there has been very little change and a typical Labour Rate for the Bodyshop is around £30 per hour or less; a significant difference.

In addition to this, the cost of labour is generally higher within a Bodyshop than it is within a Service Department because of the skills shortage and so the Labour Gross Profit is being eroded from both ends of the spectrum within the Bodyshop.

Typically, a Service Department will generate a Labour Gross Profit in excess of 80% whilst the Bodyshop maintains a figure of around 60%. The naive Manager or Accountant may compare these figures and ask why they bother with a Bodyshop, but there's many other gains to be had elsewhere.

Figure 1: Comparing Gross Profit

Service Department

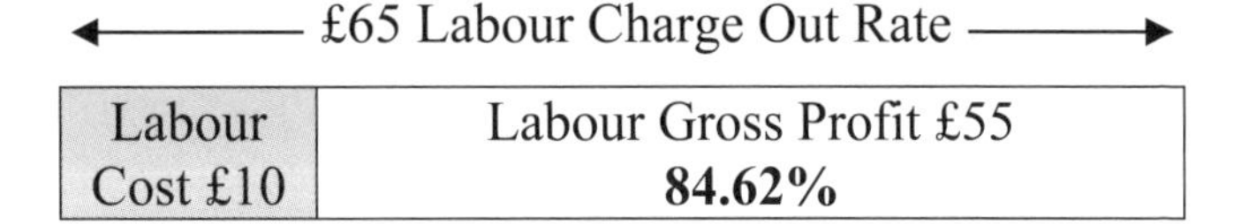

Bodyshop

← £30 Labour Charge Out Rate →

Labour Cost £12	Labour Gross Profit £18 **60.00%**

figures used for illustration purposes only.

Example calculations:

(A) Labour Rate = £30
(B) Labour Cost = £12
(C) Labour Gross Profit = £18 (A – B)
(D) Labour Gross Profit % = 60% (C ÷ A x 100)

The bad news is not all over as yet because Insurance Companies often demand high levels of discount and the Bodyshop Recovery Rate can drop from £30 per hour to as low as £23 per hour, dropping the Labour Gross profit even further.

Whilst Labour Gross Profit % may look pretty dismal in comparison, it's important to recognise that there's often a much bigger gap between the Hours Sold and the Hours Worked within a Bodyshop which means that the hourly Gross Profit % may be low, but many more hours can be sold with the selling skills or a good Estimator and therefore Productivity and the value of Gross Profit can be enhanced significantly, which is not possible within a Service Department. Therefore the main point to be taken from this section is:

Similarities and Differences

The Management Accounts and financial structure of a Bodyshop may be the same structure as a Service Department. However, the operational performance of a Bodyshop cannot be *directly* compared with a Service Department because they operate in totally different ways. They should be measured separately and without direct comparison with each other.

* * * * *

Part 1 - The Basic Business Concept of a Bodyshop
A business employs technically skilled people for a given amount of time with an hourly wage rate and also a tier of staff and management. The technically skilled people are usually know as Fitters, Panel Beaters and Painters, but for the sake of simplicity, they will be collectively described as "Operatives" within this chapter.

To understand the financial basics let's keep this example to one Operative who is employed for 8 hours per day, five days per week, with a salary of £12 per hour. It is the task of the Bodyshop to prepare an estimate for the customer and to have the Operatives working on vehicles during the time that they are at the business and to sell the hours on the estimate to its customers in order to make a profit.

Note: It is not the Operative's time that is being sold to the customers; it's the skill of the Estimator who produces the estimate for the repair that generates the Hours Sold. Operatives do not sell hours, they work them. It is the Estimator who sells the hours.

Part 2 - The Basic Terminology

The companion to this volume, The KPI Book, deals with this area much more succinctly, but for this chapter, the following terminology is in use:

Hours Bought: The total number of hours that the business will pay to an Operative, which *includes* time at the business, Holiday, Sickness and Training.

Hours Attended: The total number of hours that an Operative is at the business and is available to work on vehicles. This *excludes* Holiday, Sickness and Training.

Hours Worked: This is the total number of hours that an Operative spends clocked onto jobs, working on vehicles.

Idle Time: This is the total number of hours that an Operative is at the business, but is not clocked onto jobs. (Hours Attended minus Hours Worked.)

Hours Sold: The total number of hours that are invoiced to customers.

Recovery Rate: The amount of money that a customer is actually charged for each hour that has been sold.

Wage Rate: The amount of money that the business pays to an Operative for every hour of employment.

All of these hours are captured and coded separately on the Management Accounts so that accurate and meaningful interpretation of the figures and key performance indicators can be undertaken.

Part 3 – The Basic Structure

Now let's take a look at some activity for a simplified business called *Magnum Repairs* and set up the Management Accounts to reflect what's happening in the business. This model's simply examines labour only, other sales such as paint will be added later.

Magnum Repairs Business Activity:

A) Hours Bought	=	160
B) Hours Attended	=	140
C) Hours Worked	=	126
D) Hours Sold	=	197
E) Recovery Rate	=	£45
F) Wage Rate	=	£12
G) Other Expenses	=	£4,729

Before you continue reading, take a pen and piece of paper and create a very simple set of Management Accounts to represent these statistics. Once you've finished, you can compare your results with the example overleaf and as you continue reading, you can compare your thinking with the answers and logic that's provided throughout the rest of this chapter.

Remember at all times that this structure is very different from selling a tangible product; it's selling the value of a repair with the cost of the Operatives' time to complete the tasks in hand.

The following example illustrates how the Management Accounts need to be structured in order to reflect what is happening with labour only at an operational level within the Bodyshop:

Example 1: Management Accounts Structure for Magnum Repairs

A) Hours Bought	=	160	
B) Hours Attended	=	140	
C) Hours Worked	=	126	
D) Hours Sold	=	197	
E) Recovery Rate	=	£45	
F) Wage Rate	=	£12	
G) Other Expenses	=	£4,729	
H) Labour Sales	=	£8,865	(D x E)
I) Labour Cost of Sales	=	£1,512	(C x F)
J) Labour Gross Profit	=	£7,353	(H – I)
K) Labour Gross Profit %	=	82.94%	(J ÷ H %)
Expenses:			
L) Idle Time	=	£168	(B – C x F)
M) Holiday, Sickness Etc	=	£240	(A – B x F)
N) Other Expenses	=	£4,729	
O) Total Expenses	=	£5,137	(L + M + N)
P) Department Profit	=	£2,216	(J – O)
Q) Department Profit %	=	25.00%	(P ÷ H %)

Now let's follow the maths and logic for each of these accounting lines.

H) Labour Sales

This represents the amount of money that customers have been charged for the "labour only" content of the repairs that have been invoiced. It does not include the cost of any paint or materials that may have been charged to the customer; where applicable, Parts Sales will be shown and itemised separately. Note that the Recovery Rate is after any discount that may have been applied.

Using the *Magnum Repairs* business example, the value of the Labour Sales amounts to £8,865 which equates to the number of hours that have been sold to customers multiplied by the Recovery Rate, (D x E).

From an accounting point of view, it's very simple to show this on the Management Accounts, but from a Bodyshop Management point of view, it's really not much use because the Manager needs to know where and who the Labour is being sold to so that strengths and weaknesses can be identified. It is for these reasons that on most sets of Management Accounts, the Labour Sales are separated, at the very least, into four basic categories:

Retail Labour Sales = (General public, companies)
Internal Labour Sales = (Sales Department)
Warranty Labour Sales = (Franchise Warranty)
Insurance Labour Sales = (Insurance Companies)

As businesses grow and evolve, additional accounting lines may be added to show where the Labour Sales are coming from such as local companies or separating different Insurance companies to name but a few. The clearer the separation between categories that is shown, the more accurate the interpretation can be. These additional accounting lines do not change the complexity of the Management Accounts, in fact the opposite is true, additional information makes the business revenues easier to understand.

Important note: The number of hours sold to the customer and the amount of money charged for each hour sold is not decided or dictated by the Operatives, in other words, "*Operatives do not sell hours*", that's the job of the Estimator. The number of hours sold on the customers invoices can be higher or lower than the time it's taken the Operatives to complete the work. From an operational management point of view, there may be some time guidelines in place for the Operatives to complete the work, but from an accounting point of view there are no "*absolute*" links between the length of time that the jobs have taken and the number of hours that are sold to the customers on the Estimate.

In summary then, Labour Sales simply represents the amount of money that customers have been charged by the Estimator for the labour-only content of the Bodyshop invoices and it's influenced by their selling skills when compiling the estimate and explaining the invoices to customers.

Labour Cost of Sales

As explained in detail in Chapter VI, this is the section that causes the most confusion and complete chaos across the whole of the Motor Industry. Let's take a look at the *Magnum Repairs* example to understand the logic that's in place here.

A) Hours Bought = 160

B) Hours Attended	=	140	
C) Hours Worked	=	126	
D) Hours Sold	=	197	
E) Recovery Rate	=	£45	
F) Wage Rate	=	£12	
G) Other Expenses	=	£4,729	
H) Labour Sales	=	£8,865	(D x E)
I) Labour Cost of Sales	=	£1,512	(C x F)

The example shows Labour Sales are £8,865, but the question that remains is, "How much did it cost *Magnum Repairs* to produce that value of Labour Sales?"

The Labour Cost Of Sales is equal to the hourly rate paid to the Operatives (the wage rate) multiplied by the time it's taken the Operatives to complete those jobs, which is known as the Hours Worked. Therefore the Labour Cost of Sales is £1,512 (C x F).

Note that this is not the Operatives total salary, it represents only the portion of the Operatives salary that was paid for producing the hours that have been sold. The remainder of the monies paid to Operatives such as Idle Time, Holiday, Sickness and Training will be discussed in more detail later in the chapter.

In order for the Labour Cost of Sales to be collated accurately, the Operatives must be clocking on and off job cards and the Hours Worked must be accurately recorded on the Dealer Management System. Where automated electronic systems are not in place, the Hours Worked must be given to the

Accountant by the Bodyshop Manager because this is critical to ensure the accuracy of the output.

Common Accounting Errors

The most widespread inconsistencies appear when the Accountant and Manager do not communicate on such matters and the input varies wildly across the industry. Here are some typical examples:

Error #1- The Labour Cost of Sales is equal to the hourly rate paid to the Operatives (the wage rate), but only whilst the Operatives are present at the business, which is the Hours Attended. Therefore the Labour Cost of Sales in the Magnum Repairs example would be equal to £1,680 (B x F).

This methodology is incorrect because Idle Time would have to be reported at zero, which of course is operationally impossible. In addition to this, the Labour Gross Profit percentage would be changing after every hour had been sold because the labour cost of sales would remain constant; this would render any daily operating control completely useless.

Also this methodology would have a significant effect upon Utilisation because it would have to be reported at 100%, which renders the Manager blind to any issues surrounding workshop loading. Since Utilisation is the biggest profit builder in the Bodyshop, it obviously places the company in a disadvantageous position to have the accounts structured in this way. The Labour Cost of Sales is therefore <u>not</u> equal to the amount of money paid to the Operatives for the Hours Attended.

Error #2 - The Labour Cost of Sales is equal to the Operatives total Salary. The argument put forward here is, *"The business has to pay the Operatives total salary whether they are at work, on holiday, off sick or doing training so the whole of their salary is the Labour Cost of Sales."*

In this instance the Labour Cost of Sales in the Magnum Motors example would be equal to £1,920 (A x F). This methodology is also incorrect because it includes all of the problems listed in error #1 and it also corrupts things even further by including the cost of Holiday, Sickness and Training thereby disguising any potential problems that may exist with Operatives absenteeism. The Labour Cost of Sales is therefore <u>not</u> equal to the Operatives total salary.

Error # 3 – This is not an accounting input error, but rather a management interpretation error. Some Managers believe that the Labour Cost Of Sales is equal to the hourly rate paid to the Operatives (the wage rate) multiplied by the number of Hours Sold because that's what has been invoiced to the customer and that's how some Operatives earn their bonus. In this case the Labour Cost of Sales in the Magnum Repairs example would be equal to £2,364 (D x F). This methodology is also incorrect and is not part of any standard accounting practice; it's simply a misconception in interpretation that some Managers get drawn into.

Operational Strength and Vision
Yes, it can be argued that these so called errors are mathematically stable and from an accounting point of view they may be deemed as correct, but the

problem is that these methods leave the Manager blind to all operational performance because it's not possible to see what is happening on the workshop floor and if the Management Accounts do not provide that clear vision for the Manager, they are worthless.

There are many other permutations for what is and what is not included within the Labour Cost of Sales and whilst there may be sound logic behind each of the methodologies, from a Bodyshop Management point of view, there is only one way to make operational performance visible and controllable and that is to have the Labour Cost of Sales equal to the money that is paid to the Operatives for the number of Hours Worked. This is because it is the Hours Worked that represents the true cost of the Hours Sold and both can be controlled at an operational level by the Bodyshop Manager.

What about Operatives Bonus Payments?
Not all Bodyshops have a bonus scheme in place for Operatives and for those that do, there are many different bonus schemes and many different ways of rewarding Operatives for a job well done.

Where an Operatives bonus scheme is in place, it is usually based on the enhancement of production in some way and therefore any bonus payments made to Operatives is increasing the cost of the Hours Worked as opposed to increasing the cost of Idle Time, Holiday Sickness and Training.

In this case, bonus payment increases the cost of the Hours Worked to the company and therefore the entire bonus payment should be included within the

Labour Cost of Sales. So to have a little more clarity, the definition is extended to:

Labour Cost of Sales equal to the money that is paid to the Operatives for the number of Hours Worked, which is to include all bonus payments.

What about Operatives Overtime Payments?
This is quite simple to understand because the rules of accounting are the same. Firstly, let's define exactly what Overtime actually is. This is where an Operative is required to work outside of normal working hours and is usually paid at a higher hourly rate.

Let's say that an Operative attends 10 hours Overtime and is paid £15 per hour as opposed to the normal £12 per hour. The Operative must still clock on and off job cards whilst working Overtime and it is the Operative's time that is spent clocked onto jobs that determines the Hours Worked, which makes up the Labour Cost of Sales. The hours of Overtime that are not clocked onto jobs are classed as Idle Time.

To summarise, the treatment of Overtime is exactly the same as for normal working hours, the only difference being that Overtime is usually paid at a higher hourly rate. The effect of Overtime is that the Labour Gross Profit percentage will be reduced because the Labour Cost of Sales is now higher because the company is paying a higher Overtime rate for the Hours Worked.

Whilst working Overtime, there will undoubtedly still be a small element of Idle Time and this should be recognised as such and speaking from a Bodyshop

Management point of view, the company should not be embarking upon any Overtime if Utilisation is anywhere near or below 95%.

What About Work In Progress?
This is where work has been carried out or part carried out on vehicles but the jobs cards have not been completed. In other words, Operatives have worked on jobs and those jobs have not been invoiced as yet.

When Work In Progress (WIP) is allowed to increase the effects are that the Hours Worked will increase, but the Hours Sold will not, which means that the Labour Cost of Sales will increase in value but the Labour Sales will not. This causes a lower value to be reported in Labour Gross Profit and also the Labour Gross Profit percentage will be reduced because the Labour Sales are not reported but the Labour Cost of Sales are reported.

In addition to this distortion, high levels of Work In Progress will have a significant effect on key performance indicators. Utilisation will be seen to increase because the Hours Worked are being recorded but Productivity will be seen to decrease because the Hours Sold are not being recorded.

One critical error in handling Work in Progress is for the Hours Worked that relate to the Work In Progress to be carried forward into the next month when the jobs are invoiced. This action would show a high decline in Utilisation in the month that they were moved from and a high increase in Utilisation in the month that they were carried to. In such a case it is possible for Utilisation to be reported in excess of 100%, which is operationally impossible because that would mean that Operatives are clocked onto jobs when they are not attending the business. One of the arguments for conducting this practice is for calculating Operatives bonus payments when a time-saved bonus scheme is in place, which is calculated as follows: Hours Sold ÷ Hours Worked.

The Hours Worked are carried forward into a period to match up with the Hours Sold, but then all of the valuable data about what has really happened in the workshop has been lost and the Bodyshop Manager is left with inaccurate information upon which to make strategic decisions. The practice of moving Hours Worked from one period to another is poor accounting practice and should not be undertaken in any circumstances because it completely distorts operational performance and the ability to reshape the business for future growth.

The monetary value of the Work In Progress is shown on the Balance Sheet and the biggest factor to affect the business is cash flow. If jobs are carried out and not invoiced, the jobs cannot be converted into cash. It is for this reason that Work In Progress should be closely monitored and kept to an absolute minimum at all times.

Where Is The Operatives Salary Shown?

This is a question that is often asked and after discussing the Labour Cost of Sales, perhaps this is an appropriate juncture to explain things for the purpose of clarity.

It is a common misconception that the Labour Cost of Sales is equal to the Operatives total salary and the previous explanations have cleared up this misunderstanding. However, for simplicity, here's a straightforward list that will help to clear things up.

The Operatives salary is distributed across these six different accounting lines:

1) Labour Cost of Sales. The amount paid to the Operatives for the number of hours clocked onto jobs *(This will include Work In Progress, but will exclude the cost of Rectification and Idle Time).*

2) Rectification. The amount paid to Operatives for time spent on Rectification for the purposes of rectifying faulty work. This is an expense rather than a cost of sale, which is covered later in the chapter.

3) Idle Time. The amount paid to Operatives for the time they are at the business, but are not clocked onto jobs. There are many reasons for Idle Time, which again are covered later in the chapter.

4) Holiday. This is an expense and represents the amount paid to Operatives for the time they are on holiday. It cannot represent part of the Labour Cost of Sales because the Operatives are not available to work whilst on holiday.

5) Sickness. This is an expense and represents the amount paid to Operatives for the time they are on sick leave. It cannot represent part of the Labour Cost of Sales because the Operatives are not available to work whilst on sick leave.

6) Training. This is an expense and represents the amount paid to Operatives for the time they are on training. It cannot represent part of the Labour Cost of Sales because the Operatives are not available to work whilst training.

The proper allocation of the Operatives salary can sometimes appear to be over complicated and cumbersome to the uninitiated, but it's critical if the Bodyshop wishes to grow and develop its profitability. To function correctly, the Bodyshop Manager and the Accountant must exchange information effectively because a failure to provide the correct information to each other will produce incorrect analysis of the department.

Incorrect analysis in business is like playing a game of darts with a blindfold over your eyes – you might hit the board a few times and you may even the bulls eye once in a while, but it will not be achieved with consistency and precision.

Getting the input correct for the Hours Worked and therefore the Labour Cost of Sales is of paramount importance in understanding and controlling the available resources within the Bodyshop. Don't be tempted to take the easy route by applying the total Operatives salary into the Labour Cost of Sales because operational performance will be invisible.

Labour Gross Profit

The simple definition for this is Labour Sales minus Labour Cost of Sales, but given all of the inconsistencies that can appear in the Labour Cost of Sales, the following definition has much more clarity:

Labour Gross Profit
The invoice value of the Hours Sold
minus the amount paid to the
Operatives for the Hours Worked.

Magnum Repairs Example:

A) Hours Bought	=	160	
B) Hours Attended	=	140	
C) Hours Worked	=	126	
D) Hours Sold	=	197	
E) Recovery Rate	=	£45	
F) Wage Rate	=	£12	
G) Other Expenses	=	£4,729	
H) Labour Sales	=	£8,865	(D x E)
I) Labour Cost of Sales	=	£1,512	(C x F)
J) Labour Gross Profit	=	£7,353	(H – I)
K) Labour Gross Profit %	=	82.94%	(J ÷ H %)

The value of Labour Gross Profit (J) is affected most of all by the number of Hours Sold (D), or the volume of work that is undertaken. To a lesser degree it is also controlled by the price at which the work is sold to the customer (E) and the price paid to the Operatives for the Hours Worked (F).

It's important to note that the Labour Gross Profit % (K) is not affected by the number of Hours Sold because this is a key performance indicator that focuses only on the relationship between the buying price and the selling price of the Labour.

The Labour Gross Profit % is controlled at a Management level and is determined by the technical and selling skills of the Estimator thereby generating the Recovery Rate (E) on the Hours Sold. The other controlling aspect is the average price paid to the Operatives for the Hours Worked (F), which is affected by prices paid for standard hourly rates, bonus payments and Overtime.

Although the value of Labour Gross Profit can vary greatly from month-to-month with seasonality, the Labour Gross Profit Percentage should not be altered by this fact. Therefore controlling the operational performance and profitability of the Bodyshop can be clearly separated into very distinct levels:

1) If the value of Labour Gross Profit is too low, more work is required.

2) If the Labour Gross Profit percentage is too low, either better selling skills are required at the point of the estimate to generate more Hours Sold and a higher Recovery Rate or the price being paid to the Operatives for the Hours Worked is too high, which may be a result of bonus payments or unnecessary Overtime.

It is very important that these two areas of operational performance are not confused or merged together because it is quite possible to suffer from low sales revenues and therefore a low Labour Gross Profit value, but still have a high Labour Gross Profit percentage.

A lack of understanding in these areas of performance often causes rash and ill-conceived business decisions to be made. For instance, if the value of Labour Gross Profit is too low and the Labour Gross Profit percentage is high, the remedy is to simply obtain more work; the remedy is <u>not</u> to increase the charge out rate. However, increasing prices in an attempt to elevate profitability is a route that is often taken by the naive Bodyshop Manager and it usually ends up with a significant reduction in customer retention.

It could be that the Bodyshop does not have enough work to fulfil its objectives and increasing prices may make the situation even worse. In some instances, it may be better to create a marketing campaign where prices are reduced in an attempt to gain more work and increase customer retention. However, it is imperative that the Management Accounts are structured in a way that the effects of any such campaign are clearly visible, otherwise it's time to put the blindfold back over the Manager's eyes and get that dartboard out again.

The value of Labour Gross Profit and the Labour Gross Profit percentage are two completely different things and controlling them effectively relies upon the correct information being allocated to the Labour Cost of Sales. You can't make a good decision with bad information.

Sub-Contract

This represents jobs that are undertaken by the company, but are carried out by a 3rd party. In other words, someone else will do the work. Typical examples here might be replacement windscreens, vehicle recovery, air conditioning, tyre fitment, mechanical work and other such tasks. It is common practice for all of the tasks to be collated for the whole period and simply shown as follows:

a) Sub Contract Sales = £12,160
b) Sub Contract Cost of Sales = £9,728
c) Sub Contract Gross Profit = £2,432 (a – b)
d) Sub Contract Gross Profit % = 20% (c ÷ a x 100)

The amount of Gross Profit here will vary greatly depending upon the type of work that is undertaken. For instance, some Bodyshops have a vehicle recovery deal where they make 50% profit and other may only make 10% profit.

Also some manufacturers state that all Sub Contract work undertaken for Warranty purposes is conducted at 0% mark up, whilst other manufacturers allow a mark up of 10% to be added. In other instances, the amount of Gross Profit available on a product or service may or may not be limited and perhaps one of the biggest factors to affect the profitability is the selling skills of the Estimator, especially on retail work.

In general terms, the Sub Contract Gross Profit % to aim for is around 20%, but as already stated, there are many limiting factors that will cause it to rise and fall each month.

If the volume of Sub Contract work is consistently high, it may be worth investigating what work is being given away and whether it is possible for the company to invest in equipment to carry out this work in the future. Where this is considered, be sure to measure the investment against the possible Gross Profit to be generated to ensure a sufficient return on investment; there's no point in being a busy fool.

Paint And Materials

This is shown as a separate income stream from Labour Sales, usually with four simplified accounting lines.

Example:

a) Paint Sales	= £8,750	
b) Paint Cost of Sales	= £4,812	
c) Paint Gross Profit	= £3,938	(a – b)
d) Paint Gross Profit %	= 45.00%	(c ÷ a x 100)

Paint Sales

This captures the invoice value of all of the paint and materials that have been sold and invoiced in the given accounting period. The volume of paint sold will vary depending upon the type, mix and volume of work that is undertaken.

Paint Cost of Sales

This is simply the cost of the paint and materials that have been used in the same accounting period.

Paint Gross Profit

This is simply the invoice value of the paint sales minus the cost of the paint. The monetary value of the

Gross Profit will change with the volume of paint and materials that are sold, but the Gross Profit percentage will not change much because that key performance indicator is examining the buying price and the selling price of the paint and materials, not how much of it has been invoiced.

The Gross Profit percentage on paint and materials will vary depending upon the paint distributor and mixing systems that are in use, but typically, the paint and materials Gross Profit percentage to expect is upwards of 40%.

Parts Sales

This is where there's a significant difference between a franchised dealership and a stand-alone Bodyshop.

The franchised dealership will not show Parts Sales within the Bodyshop Management Accounts. Any parts that are sold by the Bodyshop will be shown in the Management Accounts of the Parts Department.

The stand-alone Bodyshop that is not part of a franchised dealership will show Parts Sales within the Bodyshop Management Accounts, which will of course make overall profitability comparisons difficult between a franchised Bodyshop and a stand-alone Bodyshop.

The difference in profitability made by the parts sales can be significant and is not always taken into account by the franchised dealership when conducting any assessment of the performance of its own Bodyshop and the overall profitability can sometimes be left understated.

The Management Accounts for a stand-alone Bodyshop usually show Parts sales on the four simple accounting lines.

Example:

a) Parts Sales	= £9,752	
b) Parts Cost of Sales	= £8,289	
c) Parts Gross Profit	= £1,463	(a – b)
d) Parts Gross Profit %	= 15.00%	(c ÷ a x 100)

Parts Sales
This captures the invoice value of all of the parts that have been sold and invoiced in the given accounting period. The volume and value of parts sold will vary depending upon the type and mix of work that is undertaken.

Parts Cost of Sales
This is simply the cost of the parts that have been sold in the same accounting period.

Parts Gross Profit
This is simply the invoice value of the parts sales minus the cost of those parts. The monetary value of the Gross Profit will change with the volume of parts that are sold and unlike other products that are sold, the Gross Profit percentage will also change because the buying margin on parts is not a constant factor.

This again is another area of difference between a franchised dealership and a stand-alone Bodyshop. Contrary to popular beliefs, the stand-alone Bodyshop may receive higher levels of discount from a franchised Parts Department than the integrated franchised Bodyshop within the dealership. It is the subject that receives much debate and there are of course pro's and con's to each argument (another subject for a different book).

Manufacturers pricing policies are wide and varied with higher profit margins on fast moving items and lower margins on slow moving items. Parts taken from stock have higher profit margins to those parts which are ordered on a Vehicle Off Road (VOR) basis and some parts suppliers may give higher discounts that others. All of these factors, plus the type and mix of work that is undertaken have a large effect upon the Gross Profit percentage than is achieved with Parts Sales in the Bodyshop. However, a reasonable level of Gross Profit percentage to expect on Parts Sales is upwards of 15%.

Miscellaneous / Other Sales

These are terms that hopefully are only seen on the manufacturers Composite and not on the Management Accounts of a Bodyshop. This is because they represent sales of products or services that are not individually identified.

These terms have a need to exist on a manufacturer's Composite because there needs to be a catch-all place for things that cannot be accounted for elsewhere. In other words, a dealer's Management Accounts might contain an accounting line that the Manufacturer's Composite does not contain and this is the place where the activity it can be recorded.

The downside to having this accounting line present is that it can sometimes be used as a get-out-of-jail-free card and things can get dumped here to make things balance. This is of course poor accounting practice and great concern should be voiced if there are large values placed within these accounting lines because it is not possible to know what the activity relates to and that's bad news whichever way you choose to look at it.

Departmental Gross Profit

This is a simple mathematical equation for accounting purposes and has no real operational significance. The Departmental Gross Profit is simply Total Sales minus total Cost of Sales. The Departmental Gross Profit percentage is also shown and is calculated as follows: Total Gross Profit ÷ Total Sales x 100.

From an operational perspective, the Departmental Gross Profit percentage has no real value to the Manager because the Gross Profit percentage is used to assess the performance of an individual product or service in its marketplace. Gross Profit percentage is worthless as an overall departmental figure because it averages out the profitability of all of the different products and services that have been sold. For instance, Labour Gross Profit may be 60%, Paint and Materials Sales may be at 45%, Sub Contract may be at 22%, Parts Sales may be at 16% and the combined average is... worthless.

This is because the Departmental Gross Profit percentage will change and trend up or down and the Manager will not know the reasons why by looking at this key performance indicator because all of the products and services have been merged together. This is why it is so important to begin reading

Management Accounts from the top of the page and working down rather than from the bottom of the page and working up.

When all of the products and services are merged together and then the balance of work and sales change, the departmental average will change but the Manager will be blind to any operational causes. In general terms, the Gross Profit percentage is asking the question, "How well is each individual product or service being exploited in its marketplace?" An averaged out Departmental Gross Profit percentage has no real value to the Bodyshop Manager.

Variable Expenses or Direct Expenses

This section contains a comprehensive listing of the expenses that are triggered by sales volume. They are not listed in any order of importance, some Management Accounts may even list them in alphabetical order with no preference or priority so there's no need for concern about the order of the layout, the only important factors are that they are separated from the Semi-Fixed or Indirect Expenses Let's take a closer look at some of the expenses that exist in this section.

Idle Time

This represents the amount of money paid to the Operatives for the time that is attended but not clocked onto jobs.

Here again there is a difference between a franchised dealership and a stand-alone Bodyshop. The identification of Idle Time is common practice in a Bodyshop integrated within a franchised dealership, but is not common practice within a stand-alone Bodyshop, which produces a very large blind spot for the unfortunate Manager who is tasked with improving operational performance. Let's take a look at how Idle Time is identified.

Magnum Repairs example

A) Hours Bought	=	160	
B) Hours Attended	=	140	
C) Hours Worked	=	126	
D) Hours Sold	=	197	
E) Recovery Rate	=	£45	
F) Wage Rate	=	£12	
G) Other Expenses	=	£4,729	
H) Labour Sales	=	£8,865	(D x E)
I) Labour Cost of Sales	=	£1,512	(C x F)
J) Labour Gross Profit	=	£7,353	(H – I)
K) Labour Gross Profit %	=	82.94%	(J ÷ H %)
Expenses:			
L) Idle Time	=	£168	(B – C x F)

Idle Time is at the flip side of Utilisation and is shown as a monetary value calculated by the number of hours that have been attended but not worked multiplied by the Operatives hourly rate.

There are many reasons for the accumulation of Idle Time and numerous categories on dealer management systems to assist in the identification of these weak areas. Such categories might include moving vehicles, waiting for parts, cleaning, waiting for work and many other reasons. Whilst the Management Accounts may only show a single line to report the cost of Idle Time, it is critical that the Manager has a good grasp of how these expenses have been generated. Why are Operatives being paid to attend the business, but are not clocked onto jobs?

It is important to note that Idle Time does not represent "*unsold hours*" because hours are not available to sell, hours are only available to work. Hours Sold are controlled by the Estimator and not the Operatives.

When Utilisation is increased by loading more jobs into the workshop, the Operatives will spend more time clocked onto jobs and the effect is that Idle Time will decrease and Hours Worked will increase by the same amount. This is because Hours Worked and Idle Time is simply a distribution of the Hours Attended.

Figure 2:

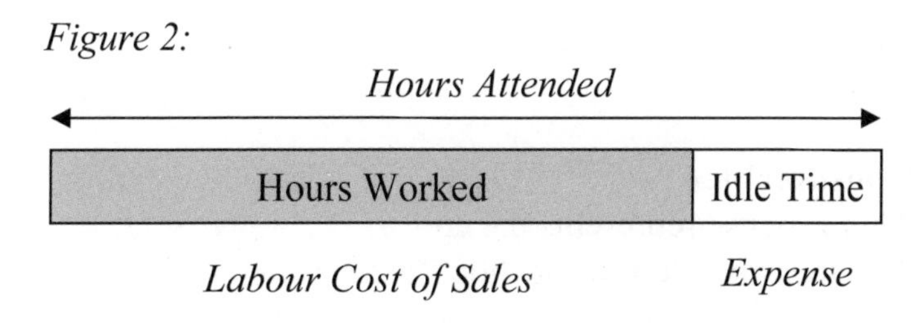

As the Hours Worked increase, Idle Time will decrease and vice versa. The objective is to keep the Operatives clocked onto jobs for as much of the Hours Attended as possible and thereby keeping the cost of Idle Time to a minimum. However, this result could be achieved by the Operatives taking a longer time to complete the same jobs, so take care to interpret the information correctly here. This is where a good understanding is needed of how Utilisation,

Productivity and Overall Efficiency work in harmony with each other.

Idle Time is shown on the Management Accounts at the cost price of Labour and therefore may not appear to be a large sum of money. However, if additional work is loaded into the workshop and then sold to the customer, it can make a significant difference to the company profitability. For instance, let's say that an additional 10 hours of work is booked into the workshop and Idle Time is therefore reduced by 10 hours. Using the Magnum Repairs figures, Idle Time would be reduced by £120 (10 hours @ £12). However, the Estimator may sell 15 hours on the invoice and the additional revenue in Labour Sales would be £675 (15 hours Sold x £45).

Idle Time may appear to be comparatively small amounts, but tapping into its potential can yield significant returns.

Consumables

This expense represents the cost of items that are used by Operatives on an ad hoc basis as they complete their work. Items here include nuts, bolts, washers, drills, releasing agent, seat covers, paper floor mats, steering wheel covers etc.

Some Bodyshops charge their customers for Consumables or Sundries and that will generate an additional accounting line within the Sales section along with Paint and Sub Contract etc. Again there will be the usual simple four lines of accounts for Sales, Cost of Sales, Gross Profit and Gross Profit%.

Introductory Commission

This represents payments made to existing customers for referring new customers to the business. A recognised and well structured referral system pays high dividends in the future growth and stability of the company and should be encouraged.

Sales Commission

This represents commissions paid to employees for selling items such as paint protection products and additional services that the company has to offer such as Smart Repairs etc.

This expense is to record commissions paid directly as a result of selling a product or a service, in other words the commission is triggered by the sale. For instance, sell one Paint Protection product, pay one commission payment. Sell two Paint Protection products, pay two commission payments and so on.

This expense line does not include any target-related bonus payments because they are shown in the line called Bonus Payments.

Miscellaneous / Other Variable Expenses

Here again we have that accounting line that should not appear within your own departmental accounts, but will appear on a manufacturers Composite. These terms have a need to exist on a manufacturer's Composite because there needs to be a catch-all place for things that cannot be accounted for elsewhere.

* * * *

Semi-Fixed Expenses or Indirect Expenses
This section contains a comprehensive listing of the expenses that are *not* triggered by sales volume. They are not listed in any order of importance, some Management Accounts may even list them in alphabetical order with no preference or priority so there's no need for concern about the layout. The important factors are that these expenses are separated from the Variable or Direct Expenses.

Salaries & Wages
This represents the basic salaries paid to the personnel of the Bodyshop who are not operatives. *(The Operatives salaries are recorded elsewhere.)*

Typically, this may include the salaries of the Bodyshop Manager, Receptionist, Estimator, Invoicing Clerk, Warranty Clerk, Foreman, Drivers, Cleaners, Vehicle Jockey, Clerical staff and any part of a Technical Expert's salary that is not included within the Hours Attended.

Target-related bonus payments made to employees are not included here.

NI & Pension
In countries where National Insurance (NI) and pension payments are made for employees, these expenses are usually shown separately to the basic salaries and sales commissions so that a fair and realistic comparison on salaries can be made.

Holiday
This expense records the salary paid to Operatives whilst they are on holiday. It cannot represent part of

the Labour Cost of Sales because the Operatives are not available to work whilst on Holiday.

Sickness
This expense records the salary paid to Operatives whilst they are on sick leave. It cannot represent part of the Labour Cost of Sales because the Operatives are not available to work whilst on sick leave. This is separated from other expenses so that any problems with absenteeism can be quickly identified.

Training Cost Salaries
This expense represents the amount of money paid to Operatives for any training that is conducted either on site at the company or off site at a training centre or college. It cannot represent part of the Labour Cost of Sales because the Operatives are not available to work whilst they are engaged in training.

An apportionment of the Apprentices salaries is also included within this expense. The most popular method in use is as follows:

Apprentice in year 1:
100% of the salary is included here because all of their time is spent with other Operatives and is classified as training.

Apprentice in year 2:
50% of the salary is included here and the other 50% is included within the Hours Attended because there is an expectation that an Apprentice in their second year will be producing work for 50% of the time that they are in attendance and therefore 50% is classed as training.

Apprentice in year 3:
25% of the salary is included here and the other 75% is included within the Hours Attended because there is an expectation that an Apprentice in their third year will be producing work for 75% of the time that they are in attendance and therefore the remaining 25% is classed as training.

Training Course Costs
This expense records the cost of the training itself as opposed to any salaries that are paid to Operatives whilst attending training. It should also include the cost of training for all Bodyshop personnel, technical or non-technical and will include training course fees, accommodation, travel and subsistence.

Bonus Payments
This relates to any target-related bonus payments that have been made to Bodyshop personnel. For instance, if the Bodyshop Manager is paid a bonus based on achieving a certain profit objective for the department, this bonus payment will be included here.

Please note any bonus payments made to Operatives are <u>not</u> included within this expense line. Bonus payments paid to Operatives should be included within the Labour Cost of Sales because those bonus payments are a reward for some form of production and therefore they should increase the cost of the Hours Worked.

Rectification
This expense is sometimes known as Goodwill, Policy Cost or Policy Adjustment. This is where an Operative has worked on a job, but the customer has

returned with a problem. The Operative will need to clock onto this job with a new job card to rectify the problem, but the customer will not be charged again.

The monetary value represents the amount paid to the Operatives for the amount of time clocked onto Rectification work. For example, if an Operative is paid £12 per hour and Rectification equates to 4 hours, the value recorded in this expense will be £48.

This is an expense that needs to be closely monitored in line with the company's right-first-time objectives because if this expense is showing an increasing trend it could be that Operative are working quickly, but taking short-cuts and compromising the task in hand.

Another indicator here is that an increasing trend could be a sign of weak Bodyshop Management, a person who cannot say "no" to non-genuine complaints. Compare the trend of this expense with any Customer Satisfaction Programmes that may be running. Having customer complaints is not a bad thing, it's how those complaints are dealt with that decides customer satisfaction and customer retention.

Computer Costs

This represents the money payable to computer maintenance contracts and equipment costs that are specific to the Bodyshop. It may also include the cost of bespoke software agreements and franchise operating systems, DMS charges, subscriptions, maintenance agreements, but it does not include the development cost of web sites because that ought to be shown as a marketing expense.

Maintenance / Equipment Costs
The represents all of the costs associated with the maintenance and repair of special tools and equipment within the Bodyshop. This will include the cost of maintaining ramps, rolling roads and heating equipment etc.

Depreciation of Equipment
This represents the amount of money that Bodyshop equipment has been depreciated.

Depreciation reduces the current value of the equipment and in doing so reduces the profitability of the department. The company therefore has a lower taxation liability. The amount of depreciation is usually decided by the Accountant, but this area is governed by Taxation Law and there are maximum limits that equipment can be depreciated within a 12 month period. Taxation Law relating to depreciation changes frequently and will be different for each country.

Warranty Write off
Where a business holds a franchise, Warranty work is undertaken by the dealer on behalf of the franchise and payment is made providing that certain criteria are followed. In the event where the criteria are not followed or an invalid Warranty claim has been made, the franchise will refuse to pay for the Warranty work undertaken. In this case, the dealer will not receive payment and will therefore have to write off the declared profit and this is the expense line where the value of the Warranty write off is shown.

Vehicle cleaning

This represents the cost of cleaning customers' vehicles after any repair or cosmetic work has been conducted. This should include the cost of all cleaning materials.

Vehicle Running Expenses

This is the total charge for the running of all vehicles in use by the Bodyshop with the exception of Courtesy Cars. Expenses here will include depreciation of the vehicles, rent or leasing payments, servicing, maintenance, road fund licence and fuel.

Courtesy Cars

This is the total charge for the running of all customer Courtesy vehicles in use by the Bodyshop. Expenses here will include depreciation of the vehicles, rent or leasing payments, servicing, maintenance, customer insurance, road fund licence, fuel and any unrecoverable road fines or expenses incurred by the customer.

Credit Card Charges

When customers pay for their work using a credit card, the company will be charged a commission by the credit card company, which is around 2% of the transaction. Taking funds on credit cards is not usually a high value transaction, but there can be many transactions so credit card charges can be rather high. Some companies charge the customer an additional 2% for payment by credit card, but this fact must be advertised in the building somewhere and it's a policy that may not contribute well towards Customer Satisfaction.

Advertising
This represents the total expenditure for the advertising and promotion of the Bodyshop, which includes direct mail, Internet campaigns and telephone marketing initiatives. Where a franchise is held, any support that is provided by the franchise should be deducted from this expense to show the true financial expenditure of the department.

General Expenses
This is the accounting line that should not appear within your own departmental accounts, but will appear on a manufacturer's Composite. These terms have a need to exist on a manufacturer's Composite because there needs to be a catch-all place for things that cannot be accounted for elsewhere. Make sure this is kept to an absolute minimum.

Total Departmental Expenses
Here again there is a big difference between a Bodyshop that is integrated within a franchised dealership and a stand-alone Bodyshop.

Firstly, in the case of the franchised Bodyshop, the total departmental expenses represent the sum total of all of the "*operational*" expenses for the Bodyshop and do not contain any of the company Overheads.

In the case of a stand-alone Bodyshop, some Accountants show the operational expenses, but also include the cost of the total business Overheads, which significantly distorts the operational analysis of the Bodyshop. This is considered to be poor accounting practice.

Recommendation For Structural Change

In the case of the stand-alone business, it is strongly recommended that the operational side of the Bodyshop activities are accounted for as a department and the Overheads are separated from operational activities and shown accordingly.

There is a very strong and compelling reason for this recommendation and it's because a Bodyshop Manager who is responsible for improving operation performance in the Bodyshop does not have any direct control over the Overheads of the company. This can have negative effects upon the motivation of the Manager because the cost of Overheads can rise outside of the Manager's control and the performance of the Bodyshop will be seen to diminish, where in fact, this may not be the case at all.

In these instances, it isn't uncommon to see Managers give up on cost control and operational performance improvement because they can feel that there is nothing they can do about it.

Simply making this structural change so that the accounting structure shows the Bodyshop as a department that is all within the control of the Manager can have a massive effect upon the mindset of the Manager and therefore operation performance. Business costs that are outside of the control of the Bodyshop Manager such as Rent, Rates and Professional Fees etcetera, should be shown separately within the company Overheads.

If company Overheads are not separated from the operational side of the business, expenses will be reported as a total figure and usually expressed as a percentage of Turnover.

Let's say that a business is reporting total Expenses as 47% of Turnover and this figure is higher than is wished for. What exactly would this figure mean and how would the Bodyshop Manager go about reducing it? The problem is that the "causes" of the expenses are not separated and merging them in this way fuses together three totally different types of expenses:

1) Departmental expenses triggered by volume
2) Departmental expenses not triggered by volume
3) Company Overheads

Which one is too high; is it all of them or just one of them?

Is the department under control and the business Overheads too high or is it the other way around?

In the case of the Bodyshop that is integrated within a franchise dealership, the total departmental expenses represent the sum total of all of the expenses for the whole of the department, which may also be expressed as a percentage of Turnover with the following calculation: Expenses ÷ Turnover x 100.

The problem here of course is that there is still a merging of operational information which leaves the Manager blind to what is happening at an operational level.

Operationally speaking, reporting a total expenses figure and producing an average is pretty worthless because the Manager will not be able to clearly see the effects of any actions that are implemented. By all means, keep an eye on this figure but pay far more attention to each expense category individually.

Direct Profit

For the Bodyshop that is integrated within a franchised dealership, this is also known as Departmental Profit, Operating Profit or more colloquially, the bottom line. This is a simple mathematical equation, which is calculated by taking the total Departmental Gross Profit, plus any bonus where applicable, minus all Departmental Expenses.

In the case of the Stand-alone Bodyshop, if company Overheads have not been separated from the departmental expenses, this factor should be taken into account.

Operationally speaking, in both cases it is of course an “effect” rather than a “cause” therefore it can only be influenced by other operational factors.

As stated in Chapter IV, it’s pointless beginning the analysis of the department here because there’s so much information that goes into it. Proper analysis of the department examines this figure last of all because it is the understanding of the individual components that make up this figure that unleashes the real power of performance improvement.

Many Management Accounts will illustrate this figure as a percentage of Turnover, but it is always the trend of this Key Performance Indicator that is of primary importance.

Magnum Repairs Example:

A) Hours Bought	=	160	
B) Hours Attended	=	140	
C) Hours Worked	=	126	
D) Hours Sold	=	197	
E) Recovery Rate	=	£45	
F) Wage Rate	=	£12	
G) Other Expenses	=	£4,729	
H) Labour Sales	=	£8,865	(D x E)
I) Labour Cost of Sales	=	£1,512	(C x F)
J) Labour Gross Profit	=	£7,353	(H – I)
K) Labour Gross Profit %	=	82.94%	(J ÷ H %)
Expenses:			
L) Idle Time	=	£168	(B – C x F)
M) Holiday, Sickness Etc	=	£240	(A – B x F)
N) Other Expenses	=	£4,729	
O) Total Expenses	=	£5,137	(L + M + N)
P) **Department Profit**	**=**	**£2,216**	(J – O)
Q) Department Profit %	**=**	**25.00%**	(P ÷ H %)

Knowing how to calculate the Direct Profit percentage is one thing, but knowing how to influence the trend is what is really required and that information is gleaned from the true understanding of both financial and commercial awareness.

The key to success with improving operational performance in the Bodyshop is to understand the relationships between Utilisation, Productivity and Overall Efficiency and have the ability to accurately forecast how these key performance indicators will change before new initiatives are implemented. The really big profit leavers are proper loading to maximise Utilisation to get more jobs through the workshop in the same time that is available and also to enhance the selling skills of the Estimator. Some Insurance companies openly state that 20% of the work that could be charged for on a job is not included on the Estimate. Is this down to selling skills, technical competence or learning how to use electronic estimating software? Many Bodyshop do not operate in the way that this chapter is suggesting and the transformation will require a concerted effort by the Accountant and the Managers. However, at a time when business Overheads are escalating and profitability is under pressure, every angle of operational performance must be closely scrutinised. Yes, it's hard work, but it may be necessary for survival in the coming years.

"The only place where success comes before work, is in the dictionary"."

- Vidal Sasson

CHAPTER XI

UNDERSTANDING THE BALANCE SHEET

"A business can survive for a long time without making a profit, but it cannot survive a single day without any cash"

- Jeff Smith

CHAPTER XI

UNDERSTANDING THE BALANCE SHEET

If there's one document in business that's much maligned, misunderstood and undervalued, it's the Balance Sheet. Skilfully compiled by Accountants and usually completely ignored by Managers, it's typically located at the back of the Management Accounts where it's treated like an outcast; discarded and uncared for. Yet it is the Balance Sheet that holds the secrets to success and it's the place where all of the power in the business resides. Those Managers who understand and can interpret the Balance Sheet are the ones who are in total control of their destiny because controlling the Balance Sheet is what makes the difference between a good business and a great business. Apart from strengthening a business, failing to understand the Balance Sheet may also weaken a business and it's usually the determining factor whether a business goes bust or not.

There's a myth surrounding the Balance Sheet which says that it's complicated and it's for the Accountant to study. Fortunately, the myth is totally unfounded because the Balance Sheet is easy to understand and it's certainly not for the exclusive use of Accountants; on the contrary, it's one of the most powerful documents a Manager will ever receive.

In brief, the Profit and Loss Account provides information relating to the products and services that have been sold, what it has cost to buy and sell those products and services and a collection of the Overheads. The Balance Sheet provides information relating to whether or not the company has been paid for those products and services and perhaps most importantly, it also assesses whether the company has enough cash to survive in the months ahead. If the company strategy involves the Managers being involved with the Balance Sheet, running the operational side of the business is relatively easy. If the company strategy does not embrace the Managers involvement with the Balance Sheet, running the operational side of the business is often very difficult and fraught with danger because these are the businesses that go bust. The Balance Sheet therefore is a very important document that is used to analyse the structure of the company and its funding arrangements.

Balance Sheet Basics

There are wide variations on the layout of Balance Sheets, but although layouts may be different, the financial structures are identical.

Essentially, the Balance Sheet is made up of two halves with one side called *Assets* and the other side called *Liabilities.*

To eradicate any confusion before it is encountered, here's a question that requires an answer *before* turning the page; the answer given must also be accompanied by a reason.

Question 1:

What is Profit, is it a Liability or an Asset?

Possible Answers Given:

1) Profit is an Asset because Assets are positive and Liabilities are negative.

2) Profit is an Asset because an Asset means that you own something and you own profit

3) Profit is an Asset when you have made a profit and a Liability when you have made a loss.

4) Profit is a good thing, so it must be an Asset.

5) Profit cannot be Liability because it just doesn't sound right.

6) Profit is a Liability because you always have to make profit.

7) Profit can be both a Liability and an Asset, it depends whether the company has a bank overdraft or not.

8) It's a trick question, profit is neither a Liability nor an Asset.

Whilst these answers all sound plausible, in fact none of them are correct and that's because of the meaning that's placed on the words Asset and Liability.

To clear things up and eradicate any confusion, let's first replace these words with other words that are less ambiguous in their meaning, the first two replacement words are In and Out.

Replace the word "Asset" with the word "out". To put it another way, Assets represent funds that go "out" of the company.

Now replace the word "Liability" with the word "in". To put it another way, Liabilities represent funds that come "in" to the company.

Now the answer to the question is more clearly visible. Profit comes "in" to the company therefore profit is a Liability.

But wait a minute...Profit is a Liability; that just does not sound right, does it? Profit is a Liability and it should therefore be avoided at all costs – it sounds crazy! The reason that people think this way is because they see themselves and the company as the same entity.

Imagine for a moment that you are the Managing Director of a company and you own all of the shares. The company makes a profit of £100,000 and the question is, to whom does that profit belong?

The answer is that the profit belongs to you because you own all of the shares. However, where is that profit right now?

The answer is that the profit is held by the company.

Now here's the bit that makes sense of it all. The company is holding the profit, but the profit belongs to you, therefore at some point in time, the company has to pay that profit to you. Therefore the profit is a Liability to the company. The critical point of understanding here is that you and the company are two completely separate entities.

Now that's cleared up, let's introduce two more replacement words that are better suited to our needs; Source and Use. Liabilities are a *Source* of funds and Assets are a *Use* of funds. Just to confirm, profit is a Liability because it is a source of funds, it comes into the company.

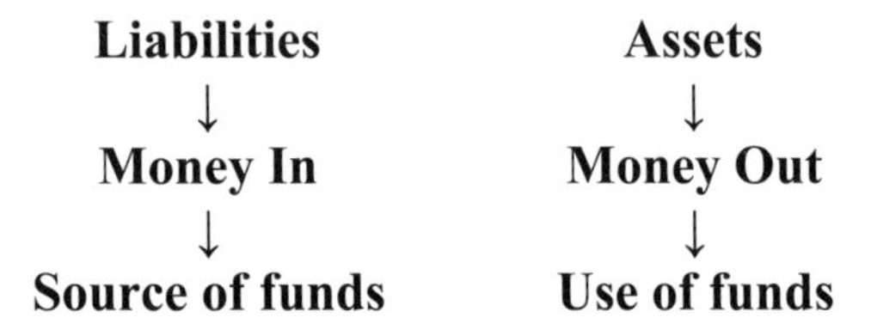

Now let's take a closer look at how Balance Sheets are displayed. In its most simple format the Balance Sheet is laid out as above with Liabilities on the left and Assets on the right. However, the French methodology would see these reversed with Assets on the left and Liabilities on the right. Neither way is right nor wrong, they're just different layouts.

In the early days of Accounting, all Balance Sheets were displayed in this left/right manner and it is only in recent times that the layouts have changed to display all of the information in a single column. This columnar style of Balance Sheet usually shows the Assets in the top half of the column with the Liabilities contain within the bottom half. However, it would also be acceptable to display the Liabilities in the top half and the Assets in the bottom half.

Figure 1: The Right/Left Style

Liabilities	**Assets**
Where funds have come from	Where funds have gone to

Figure 2: The Columnar Style

Assets
Where funds have gone to
Liabilities
Where funds have come from

The columnar style is a better format for trending multiple months of data because it's simple to add another column to the right. However, the Right/Left style is better for seeing the movement of funds, but it not as efficient for trending multiple months of data.

It is for these reasons that the most common format nowadays is the columnar style of Balance Sheet because it's a much more efficient page layout and much more suitable for manufacturers Composites and other comparative data. Because of the ease of visibility, the left/right style of Balance Sheet will be used in this chapter.

What Is A Balance Sheet?

A Balance Sheet is produced at the end of each month and is a snapshot of the company's financial status. It shows where all the money has come from and where that money has been spent.

A Balance Sheet must always balance because it is a record of the movement of the same money; it cannot do anything else but balance, here's an example:

Figure 3: The House

Liabilities		Assets	
Deposit Mortgage	£100k £400k	House	£500k
Total Liabilities	£500k	Total Assets	£500k

In this very simple example above, a house has been purchased for £500k. That's what the funds have been spent on therefore the house is an Asset. However, where did the £500k come from to purchase the house?

This is where the Liabilities come into play. The funds came from a deposit of £100k and a Mortgage of £400k.

The Balance Sheet balances because it's displaying the same money. It's showing where £500k came from to buy the house and where the money has gone to, the house itself. That's it, it's as easy as that!

Balance Sheet Terminology And Definitions
A company Balance Sheet contains many more items than the very simplified model in *figure 3*, however, the financial principles are exactly the same. Let's take a closer look at the different components of a Balance Sheet and then explain them in a more detail.

Figure 4: Components Of A Balance Sheet

<table>
<tr><th>Liabilities</th><th>Assets</th></tr>
<tr><td>Net Worth</td><td rowspan="2">Fixed Assets</td></tr>
<tr><td>Loan Capital</td></tr>
<tr><td></td><td></td></tr>
<tr><td>Current Liabilities</td><td>Current Assets</td></tr>
<tr><td>Total Liabilities</td><td>Total Assets</td></tr>
</table>

The model above shows that there are 5 different components to a Balance Sheet, those being Fixed Assets, Current Assets, Current Liabilities, Loan Capital and Net Worth. This model has a shaded line across the centre of the Balance Sheet creating an upper and lower section.

A Balance Sheet separates its contents by Source and Use and also by long-term and short-term. In the case of the Balance Sheet, short-term means from this point forward up to 12 months ahead and long-term simply means any period longer than 12 months ahead.

Fixed Asset
This represents a use of funds that is invested in something for a period of *more* than 12 months. The term has nothing to do with values being fixed, nor does have anything to do with the asset itself being fixed in position. It's something that the company has purchased and the funds will remain tied up in the asset for longer than one year. Otherwise known as a long-term investment.

Current Asset
This represents a use of funds that are invested in something for a period of *less* than 12 months. In other words, this represents something that the company buys and intends to sell within a period of one year or less. Otherwise known as a short-term investment.

What's The Difference In Assets?
The difference between Fixed Assets and Current Assets depends upon the "*intention*" of how the assets are going to be used. For instance, used vehicles are classified as a Current Asset because the "*intention*" is to buy and sell the used vehicles within 12 months (hopefully 90 days or less).

In some extreme instances, a used vehicle might remain in stock for more than 12 months, but this does not change its classification to a Fixed Asset because the Balance Sheet is looking forward 12 months from the date it's produced. Therefore no matter how long a used vehicle remains in stock, it's always the "*intention*" of the business to sell the used vehicles in the next 12 months, therefore they are always classified as a short-term use of funds.

Vehicles do appear in Fixed Assets, but those are not the ones that the business intends to sell in the next 12 months. Typically these vehicles might include recovery vehicles, delivery vehicles or other company vehicles used by the Directors that are not for sale. The monies tied up in these vehicles will be there for longer than 12 months therefore it's classified as a long-term use of funds.

What's The Difference In Liabilities?

Essentially, there are three types of Liabilities and just as the Assets are divided by the "*intention*" of a 12 month time principle, so too are the Liabilities. However, there is one small difference. Some of the Liabilities are classified as short-term (less than 12 months), some are classified as long-term (more than 12 months) and the third category is classified as permanent funds. Let's begin with this third category.

Net Worth

This is the part of the company that represents the owner's funds or the shareholders funds. It is made up of the initial cash that was introduced to start the business and other funds that have been earned during its life such as accumulated profits. It's often referred to as "permanent funds" because the funds held here are not normally repayable during the life of the company and will remain in place until the company is eventually sold.

Loan Capital
This category represents the sources of funds that must be repaid by the company after the current 12 month period; the company's long-term loans. These may be borrowings such as the mortgage on the property, hire purchase agreements on equipment and any other loans that have a repayment length or more than one year. This could be 2 years or 20 years, long-term just means more than 12 months.

Current Liability
These are the company's short-term borrowings. In other words, these are the funds that have been borrowed from various sources that the company "*intends*" to repay within the current 12 months. This could be anywhere between 24 hours and one year. Items in this section might include the Bank Overdraft and suppliers of goods and materials.

So What's The Point?
A Balance Sheet comprises of a listing of the company's financial status; a "Statement of Affairs". The Liabilities show where the company has obtained its funds from and how soon they have to be repaid. The Assets show where those funds have been used within the company and how long those funds will be tied up. All of these factors are important because it's critical to maintain the correct level of funding in each category; *it's by no means random*. Set up the Balance Sheet correctly and running the company on a day-to-day basis is relatively easy and straightforward. Failure to set up the Balance Sheet correctly significantly increases the chances of the company going bust.

Figure 5: Balance Sheet Summary

<table>
<tr><th>Liabilities</th><th>Assets</th></tr>
<tr><td>Net Worth
Long-Term Source
Permanent</td><td rowspan="2">Fixed Assets
Long-Term Use
More than 1 year</td></tr>
<tr><td>Loan Capital
Long-Term Source
More than 1 year</td></tr>
<tr><td></td><td></td></tr>
<tr><td>Current Liabilities
Short-Term Source
Less than 1 year</td><td>Current Assets
Short-Term Use
Less than 1 year</td></tr>
<tr><td>**Total Liabilities**</td><td>**Total Assets**</td></tr>
</table>

This chapter is written as an introduction to the Balance Sheet rather than a full blown interpretation of all of the key performance indicators and how to set up a company correctly. However, there are three factors that simply cannot be ignored if this book is to have any credibility and they are all concerning the most important factor of any organisation, which is cash flow.

Understanding Working Capital

If a company were a human being, its working capital would be its blood supply. A Doctor measures the blood pressure in the human body to ensure that it is at the correct level. If blood pressure is too high the body begins to haemorrhage and if it is too low the patient will die. Just as it is the Doctor's job to control and regularly measure a patient's blood pressure, it is the Manager's job to control and regularly measure the company's Working Capital.

Net Worth, Loan Capital and Fixed Assets all contain long-term funds and therefore show little change as time passes. However, the Current Liabilities and the Current Assets are where the company's trading activities are seen to be taking place. These are the parts of the Balance Sheet where the company's Managers are funding the processes of buying and selling products and services on a day-to-day basis; it's the part of the business that's "working".

Figure 6: Identifying Working Capital

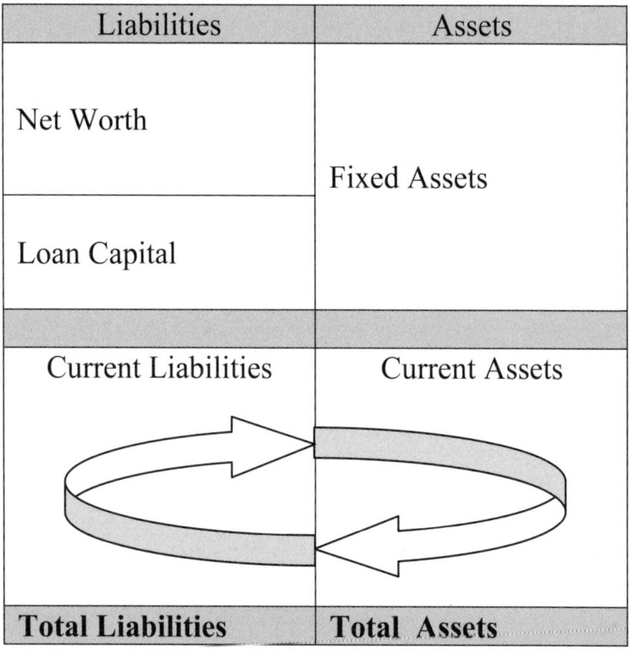

Liabilities	Assets
Net Worth	Fixed Assets
Loan Capital	
Current Liabilities	Current Assets
Total Liabilities	**Total Assets**

To calculate the value of Working Capital within a company, the formula is simply Current Assets minus Current Liabilities. This formula will provide a monetary value, but by itself, the monetary value doesn't really mean much at all until it's put into the right context.

Just as a human body needs just the right amount of blood to function properly, a business needs just the right of Working Capital to function properly, but the question is, how much Working Capital does a business need? The Answer lies in a key performance indicator known as Current Ratio.

How Much Working Capital Is Required?
Perhaps the logical answer to this question is, "as much as possible to allow flexibility". However, this is totally incorrect because there's no point investing funds into a company that are not going to be utilised because that would reduce the company's Return on Investment. The answer is to keep Working Capital to as small amount as possible, but the problem is, if there's not enough, the company will go bust.

It is for these reasons that Current Ratio is the number one key performance indicator to manage, monitor and control in any business because it assesses whether a company has the right amount of Working Capital to survive.

The formula for calculating Current Ratio is Current Assets divided by Current Liabilities. Once calculated it will produce a number such as 1.27 or something similar. The number seen is a ratio and would be reported as 1.27:1. This ratio means that the Current

Assets are 1.27 times greater than the Current Liabilities, or in other words, for every £1 that is borrowed in Current Liabilities, there is £1.27 invested in Current Assets.

Example:

a) Current Assets	=	£952,500	
b) Current Liabilities	=	£750,000	
c) Working Capital	=	£202,500	(a – b)
d) Current Ratio	=	1.27:1	(a ÷ b)

The benchmark to maintain for Current Ratio is between 1.25:1 and 1.30:1 which is a very narrow window of tolerance with little or no room for error. This is because the Motor Industry is a very money-hungry business and cash has a tendency to go out at a faster rate than it comes in and this is a situation that is of paramount importance. Survival in business is not determined by the company's Net Profit %, survival is determined by the company's ability to manage the right levels of Working Capital.

When Current Ratio rises above 1.30:1 it's an indicator that there is too much Working Capital invested in the company and as a result there will be a tendency to see overage used vehicles, poor credit control and low stock turns. It's only a matter of time before these practices bring a once successful company down to its knees.

When Current Ratio falls below 1.25:1 this is a severe warning signal that the company will soon begin to encounter cash flow difficulties and restrictions will be placed upon day-to-day trading making things even worse.

Controlling Working Capital by maintaining Current Ratio at the correct levels is perhaps *THE* most important responsibility that can be placed upon a management team. Attempting to operate a company and implementing actions without knowing the effects of those actions upon Current Ratio is nothing less than commercial Russian roulette.

Cash flow problems rarely occur overnight, they occur over a period of time and the warning signs can be clearly seen from the outset when Current Ratio is tracked and trended each month.

When Current Ratio is in decline, immediate action is required because it's much easier to stay out of trouble than it is to get out of trouble.

There is an action that wreaks havoc and often causes a business to go bust and it's called an Imbalance of Funds.

An Imbalance of Funds

Learning by paradox is often a good thing because knowing what *not* to do in business might just save the company from a commercial disaster that ends up with insolvency or foreclosure.

The previous sections have demonstrated the absolute importance of monitoring and controlling Working Capital, but when a management team does not understand or is not in control of Current Ratio, it's possible to create an Imbalance of Funds and everything comes crashing down.

An Imbalance of Funds occurs when the wrong type of funding is used to purchase assets. For instance, long-term investments are financed with long-term loans and short-term investments are financed with short-term loans. An Imbalance of Funds is when short-term loans are used for long-term investments.

Figure 7: An Imbalance of Funds

Liabilities	Assets
Net Worth	Fixed Assets *Long-Term Investment*
Loan Capital	
Current Liabilities *Short-Term Funds*	Current Assets
Total Liabilities	**Total Assets**

An Imbalance of Funds has the same effect on a business as kryptonite does to Superman. It strips it of all of its power and brings the company to its knees.

Knowing that maintaining the correct amount of Working Capital is critical to survival in business, it's possible to see from figure 7 that when short-term funds are used to finance long-term investments, the action strips away Working Capital by reducing the Current Liabilities, which may leave the company struggling for cash to fund the stocks and trading activities. Let's use the previous example to demonstrate this fact.

Example prior to Imbalance of Funds:

a) Current Assets	=	£952,500	
b) Current Liabilities	=	£750,000	
c) Working Capital	=	£202,500	(a – b)
d) Current Ratio	=	1.27:1	(a ÷ b)

Now conduct the Imbalance of Funds by purchasing £50,000 worth of equipment in Fixed Assets with funds taken from the Current Liabilities, which might be the Bank Overdraft for instance.

Effects after the Imbalance of Funds:

a) Current Assets	=	£952,500	(remains static)
b) Current Liabilities	=	£800,000	(+ £50,000)
c) Working Capital	=	£152,500	(a – b)
d) Current Ratio	=	1.19:1	(a ÷ b)

The benchmarks for Current Ratio are between 1.25:1 and 1.30:1 so with Current Ratio now being reported at 1.19:1 this means that the company no longer has enough Working Capital for its day-to-day trading activities. This is obviously catastrophic because the company will be *forced* to make changes at an operational level because it's running out of cash.

In franchised dealerships, the Sales Departments will not be able to conduct corporate business because the company no longer has the cash to fund the outstanding debt for 14 days or more, bonuses are not achieved, profitability falls and cash flow is hit even further. The uneducated Manager usually responds to this lack of cash by liquidating used vehicle stock, but that's the worst thing to do because the Manager is treating the symptoms, not the disease. The problem has not been caused by the used vehicle stock, the problem has been caused by the Imbalance of Funds.

Once the used vehicle stock is liquidated there is a slight reprieve because some cash will come in to the company, however, the business has less stock to sell and therefore less chance to generate more profit in order to recover.

From this point forward everything gets worse because restrictions are constantly being placed upon the Managers ability to trade due to the lack of cash. Parts Department Trade accounts are restricted and parts sales diminish. Service Department accounts are restricted, customer satisfaction falls and customer retention diminishes. Bodyshops don't have the funds to purchase parts, they've been put on stop by their suppliers and productivity diminishes. It's only a matter of time before the business enters foreclosure.

The sad part in all of this is that a well performing business can implode upon itself and go bust – not because it has forgotten how to sell products and services to make a profit, but because it has run out of cash due to a catastrophic and fundamental error known as an Imbalance of Funds.

Looking from this privileged view, it's easy to see *what* solution should have been applied and *when* it should have been applied.

The correct solution would have been to arrange a £50,000 long-term loan to fund the £50,000 long-term investment in the equipment. If that had been arranged at the time that the equipment was purchased, the £50,000 would not have been wiped out of the Working Capital and the Managers would not have been subjected to any restrictions.

"A business can survive for a long time without making a profit, but it cannot survive a single day without any cash"

In the example, a sum of £50,000 was used to show the Imbalance because it's a large amount of money and the point is easily seen. In real life, the amounts might not be quite so high on individual transactions, but they can accumulate to this kind of value over the period of a year. For instance, a franchise might insist that a new diagnostic machine is required as part of the operating standards and it gets delivered with an invoice for £5,000 which will be debited from the company's sundries account in 3 days time. The uneducated Manager has a moan at the franchise, but allows the transaction to take place.

In this instance, alarm bells should ring and the appropriate long-term loan should be sourced immediately to fund the equipment. If the funds are taken from the bank account, that's £5,000 instantly wiped out of the Working Capital. The pain may not be too great at this early stage, but what happens in 12 months time when 7 or 8 such transactions have happened? These may be things such as a new diagnostic machine for the workshop, new display stands for the showroom or Parts Department, new gas recharging machine for air conditioning units, new equipment for smart repairs in the Bodyshop and perhaps the biggest offender of all, new signage and corporate identity for the building.

Over this period of time the business will have lost tens of thousands in Working Capital and the process of liquidating stock begins. After another 2 years or so, sales volumes will have increased, prices will have increased and the demand for cash is higher. However, it's not available because it's all been spent on long-term investments that are not cash generating items and the business will go bust.

An Imbalance of Funds is to be avoided at all costs because it ravages through Working Capital with the alacrity and ruthless efficiency of a plague of Locusts on a field of crops leaving a trail of barren destruction in its wake. Use short-term funds for short-term investments and use long-term funds for long-term investment. The golden rule is:

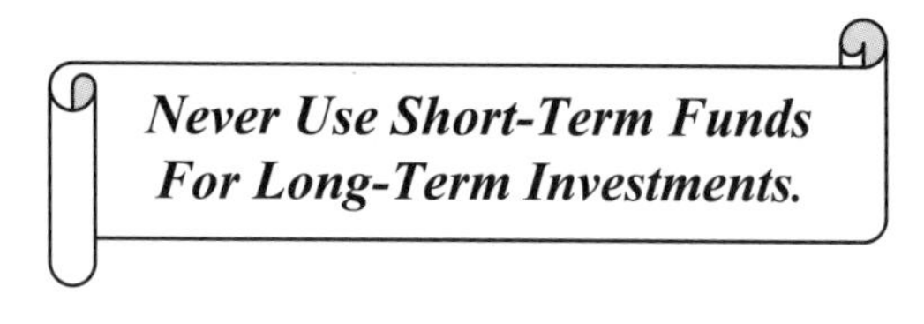

* * * * *

Fixed Assets
This section contains many of the Fixed Assets that may be found on a Balance Sheet, they are listed in no particular order of importance. Some definitions are self explanatory whilst others are not quite so obvious.

Land and Buildings
Where the land and Buildings are freehold or owned by the company, this represents the net book value of the land and building. Where the properties are rented or leased, this is known as "off Balance Sheet Funding" and the rental payment will be found within the company Overheads.

Property Improvements
This relates to any capital expenditure spent on the property such building extensions but excludes maintenance costs.

Plant and Equipment
This is the current net value of the things such as workshop ramps, workshop equipment, computer hardware systems, Bodyshop oven and Jig.

Fixtures and Fittings
These are often included within Plant and Equipment and include the current net value of the things such as desks, chairs, office equipment and telephones etc.

Company Vehicles
This is the current value of all vehicles that are in use by the company where they will be used for a period of more than 1 year. This will exclude demonstrators and courtesy vehicles.

Goodwill

This is an accounting term that normally arises only in the case of an acquisition. It's used to reflect the fact that when the business was purchased, it had an intrinsic value beyond the value of its assets, such as the reputation the company or a long standing customer base. When purchasing a business that already exists, a buyer may have to pay an amount of Goodwill to the seller which is a value that is mutually agreed between the two parties. The value of Goodwill on the Balance Sheet is the total price paid for the company minus the net book price of the total assets.

* * * * *

Current Assets

This section contains many of the Current Assets that may be found on a Balance Sheet, they are listed in no particular order of importance. Some definitions are self explanatory whilst others are not quite so obvious. Current Assets is the place where the company's stock is located.

Debtors

This is where the company has sold and invoiced its products and services to its customers, but has not yet received payment; the cash is still outstanding to the company. Within the Motor Industry, Debtors may be sub divided in to further categories:

Debtors - Vehicles

The monies owed to the company for sold and invoiced vehicles. The money may be outstanding from finance companies or fleet companies with extended credit terms. This is one area that soaks up inordinate amounts of cash and causes one of the biggest problems when the company commits the wrongful act of creating an Imbalance of Funds. When there is insufficient Working Capital, fleet business is unattainable or it is the thing that causes the business to go bust. Great care should be taken when agreeing corporate deals on new vehicles to ensure that the Working Capital in use here is not stifling the growth of the company by preventing other parts of the company to operate effectively.

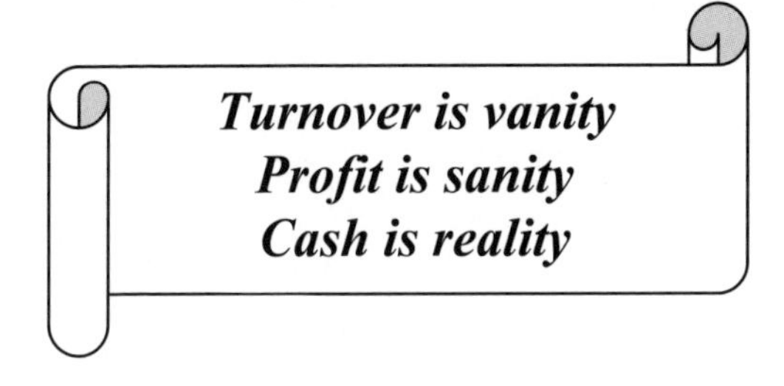

Debtors - Trade

This is the monies outstanding from normal day-to-day trading activities in the business. It represents credit given to the customers of the Service Department, Parts Department and Bodyshop. The values are usually much smaller than can be seen in vehicle debtors, but the amounts are usually outstanding for much longer periods of time. Debtors over 45 days old are unacceptable because the older the debt, the less likely it is to be collected. This is a very important area that requires investigation and action on a weekly basis. Customers who do not pay their invoices within the agreed repayment timescales are not good customers for the business because they cause cash flow problems. It is far better to let these customers go elsewhere and leave your business in a healthy position than to retain customers who do not pay and have your business eventually go bust. Sometimes you have to lose a battle to win the war.

Debtors - Warranty
Where a business holds a franchise, this represents the value of the parts and labour invoiced to warranty that has not yet been paid by the franchise. Aged debt here is caused by poor warranty procedures and late submissions.

Debtors - Franchise
This represents monies owed to a franchised dealership by the franchise or manufacturer. It will include bonuses that have been earned by the business, but have not yet been paid. Typically, these bonuses will include target-related volume bonus, CSI bonus and dealer standards.

Used Vehicles
This represents the total value of all used vehicles that are currently held in stock. The value is the stand in value (SIV) of the vehicles after any over allowance, write back and depreciation has been deducted.

New Vehicles
This is the total cost of any new vehicles that have been adopted or fully paid by the company and does not include any vehicles that are on consignment from the franchise.

Generally speaking, new vehicles are supplied to a business on a consignment basis which means that the business does not have legal title to the vehicles, but is liable to pay interest charges, which is shown in the company Overheads. Usually, the consignment period is around 180 days after which time the vehicle is adopted by the business and the vehicle is paid in full.

New vehicle stock that is fully paid is really bad news and should be avoided at all cost because it absorbs working capital unnecessarily. Appropriate systems should be in place to prevent any new vehicles from approaching the end of a consignment period. It is better to sell these vehicles at a loss rather than to pay for them in full and continue to pay interest charges on them.

Any value present in this section of the Balance Sheet illustrates poor practices in Sales Management.

New Vehicles on Consignment

Vehicle consignment is the act of a franchise placing new and unregistered vehicles in the hands of their dealer network, but retaining ownership until the vehicles are sold.

This heading is usually not included on a dealer's Balance Sheet because the dealer does not have legal title to the vehicles therefore they are not an asset of the company. However, a franchise may request inclusion of these vehicles for their Composite input in order to create a level playing field for comparison across a dealer network.

Where this inclusion is the case, the value of consignment stock will be offset to the same value by a New Vehicle Consignment Stocking Loan within the Current Liabilities to enable the Balance Sheet to balance.

The inclusion of consignment vehicles in the Current Assets and its corresponding loan in the Current Liabilities will cause Current Ratio to decrease therefore reporting a lower level of Working Capital than is really the case. The size of the distortion upon Current Ratio will be determined by the value of the vehicles on consignment.

Demonstrator Vehicles

This is the value of all vehicles held in stock for the purposes of demonstration. It represents the net value of the vehicles plus taxation (VAT) and should include the cost of any additional accessories fitted and should be net of depreciation. Any outstanding values on finance for these vehicles will be shown within the Current Liabilities as Demonstrator Finance.

Parts Stock

This represents the net book value of the total parts that are held in stock at cost price less any provision that has been made for obsolescence. Some franchises may request this information split between franchise parts and non-franchise parts for Composite input.

Work In Progress

This represents the cost of parts and labour on work carried out in the Service Department and Bodyshop that has not yet been invoiced. When the jobs are complete they will be invoiced and either the cash will be collected or it will appear as a Debtor.

Prepayments

Contrary to what many people think, this is not where a customer pays the company a deposit or makes a prepayment for a vehicle; it's is the opposite of this. A Prepayment is where the company itself pays in advance of receiving a product or a service. An example of this might be an Insurance premium that is paid annually in advance.

Cash

This is a Current Asset because it's like a stock of money being used as either cash in hand or cash held at the bank.

* * * * *

Current Liabilities

This section contains many of the Current Liabilities that may be found on a Balance Sheet, they are listed in no particular order of importance. Some definitions are self explanatory whilst others are not quite so obvious. Current Liabilities is the place where the company has its short-term loans that are used to funds its stocks.

Bank Overdraft

Unlike other loans, there is no agreed time limit when the Bank Overdraft is to be repaid. However, it is regarded as a short-term loan because the Bank can demand full payment of this loan at any time. If the company does not operate with a Bank Overdraft, this will have a value of zero and the cash that is being held in the Current Account will be shown on the other side of the Balance Sheet under Current Assets.

Stocking Loans

These are loans that are specifically related to stock. For instance, it is common practice for a finance company to provide a credit line for the specific use of used vehicle stock.

Where this is the case, a Representative from the finance company will assess and value the used vehicle stock on a monthly basis and provide a credit facility of up to 80% of the used stock value.

Let's say that the used vehicle stock is valued at £100,000 then the credit facility offered by the finance company would be a maximum of £80,000 and the business would fund the remaining £20,000 from the Bank Overdraft.

Other specific stocking loans may be in existence for Demonstrator Vehicles and Courtesy Vehicles.

Loan Repayments

This represents the amount of a loan that is repayable in the current 12-month period. For instance, if a company arranges a loan for £100,000 over a period of 10 years, the loan repayment would be £10,000 because that is the amount of the total loan that is due for payment in the next 12 months.

Example:

a) Loan Amount	£100,000	
b) Loan Term	10 Years	
c) Loan Repayment	£10,000	(a ÷ b)

The Balance Sheet will not itemise all of the different loans that have been taken out, it simply shows the total amount payable in loan repayments in the next 12 months. *(Also see Loan Capital)*

Note: Interest charges are not shown on the Balance Sheet, they are shown within Company Overheads as an expense.

Creditors
This is where the company has received products, services and raw materials from its suppliers, but has not yet paid for them. The company "intends" to pay its suppliers within the current 12-month trading period (usually 30 days credit is given) and is therefore classified as a short-term loan.

Where a franchise is held, this usually represents the monies owed by the business to the franchise for parts purchases.

Trade Creditors
This will be the monies owed to suppliers for the provision of products, services and raw materials that have been purchased from sources other than the franchise. This may include OEM parts suppliers, oil and all other purchases such as stationery etc where a period of credit is given to the company.

Directors Loans
Contrary to popular thought, these are not loans provided by the company to its Directors, in fact it is the opposite. This is where the Directors provide a loan to the company.

For instance, let's say that a Director has an annual salary of £100,000 but at this particular time, the company is experiencing some difficulties with cash flow. The Director may decide to take only a portion of the salary and leave the rest in the company for a period of time to assist with cash flow. The Director intends to take the remainder of the salary when the company can afford to do so.

Example:

a) Directors Salary	£100,000	
b) Salary Taken	£60,000	
c) Directors Loan	£40,000	(a – b)

The Director has left £40,000 in the company to assist with the cash flow problems, but the fact that the money is shown within the Current Liabilities means that the Director "intends" to take that £40,000 out of the company within the next 12 months.

If the company recovers from its cash flow problems, all is well and good, the Director will take the salary and the Directors Loan will not be evident. However, if the company does not recover from its cash flow problems and subsequently approaches a Bank for additional loans, the Bank Manager will insist that the Directors Loan is removed from Current Liabilities. This is because the Bank will not provide a loan to the company only for the Director to take it out as salary; the funds must remain within the company.

Accruals

When a company knows that a debt is payable in the future but has not yet received an invoice or demand for that debt, it creates an accrual for the amount that is due. In other words, an accrual is a financial "recognition" of a future debt that must be paid out, but has not yet been invoiced by a supplier.

* * * * *

Loan Capital

This section represents the long-term portion of all loans the company has taken for which repayments will be made outside of the next 12 months. The part of the loan that is due within the next 12 months is found within Current Liabilities identified as Loan Repayments.

Understanding Loans

When a company arranges a loan, some of the loan is repayable within the next 12 months and the remaining balance is due after 12 months. Here's an example of how a loan for £10,000 over a period of 5 years is shown on the Balance Sheet.

Example:

a) Total Loan Amount	£10,000	
b) Loan Term	5 Years	
c) Payment due in current year	£2,000	(a ÷ b)
d) Payment due after 1 year	£8,000	(a – c)

This is how the loan would be structured on the Balance Sheet when it is first taken out. The total £10,000 loan is not shown a one place, it's shown in two different places to shown how much is due in the current year and how much is due after one year.

The Loan Capital section of the Balance Sheet only captures the value of the loans that are due to be paid after 1 year.

As time passes, loan repayments are made and the amount due on the loan is therefore reduced. However, the Balance Sheet is always looking at the next 12 months ahead therefore when repayments are made, the Loan Repayments shown within the Current Liabilities remain at the same value because that value is due within the *next* 12 months and the value shown in the long-term loan is reduced by the value of the loan repayment. Here's how it works:

Figure 8:

	Year 1	Year 2	Year 3	Year 4	Year 5
Long Term	8,000				
Short Term	2,000				

In figure 8 above, year 1 shows that £2,000 is due to be paid in Loan Repayments within the next 12 months (short-term) and £8,000 is due to be paid after 12 months (long-term). When added together, the total outstanding loan is £10,000.

Figure 9:

	Year 1	Year 2	Year 3	Year 4	Year 5
Long Term	8,000	6,000			
Short Term	2,000	2,000			

Year 2 shows that £2,000 is due to be paid in Loan Repayments within the *next* 12 months and £6,000 is due after 12 months. When added together, the total outstanding loan has been reduced to £8,000. This is because Loan Repayments of £2,000 were made in year 1.

Figure 10:

	Year 1	Year 2	Year 3	Year 4	Year 5
Long Term	8,000	6,000	4,000		
Short Term	2,000	2,000	2,000		

Year 3 shows that £2,000 is due to be paid in Loan Repayments within the *next* 12 months and £4,000 is due after 12 months. When added together, the total outstanding loan has been reduced to £6,000. This is because a Loan Repayment of £2,000 was made in year 1 and a further Loan Repayment of £2,000 was made in year 2.

Figure 11:

	Year 1	Year 2	Year 3	Year 4	Year 5
Long Term	8,000	6,000	4,000	2,000	0
Short Term	2,000	2,000	2,000	2,000	2,000

The illustration above shows the complete cycle of the loan over a 5 year period. When loan repayments are made, it is the values of the long-term loans within Loan Capital that are reduced because the Balance Sheet will be recreated and the company will always have loan repayments due to be paid over the *next* 12 months until the loan is fully paid.

Long-Term loans might include mortgages on the property and hire purchase agreements on plant, equipment and company vehicles.

Net Worth
These are the funds in the company that are in for the duration, in other words, these funds will remain in place until the company is sold hence they are sometimes referred to as permanent funds.

Share Capital
This is the amount of set-up capital that is put into a limited company by the Directors/shareholders when the company first began its life. The value of Share Capital can be increased at a later date, but this is a rare occurrence because the Directors usually secure loans to inject more capital into the company rather than putting more capital in themselves.

Understanding Reserves
Throughout the Profit & Loss Account, each department generates a profit (or a loss) after selling its products and deducting its expenses. The Overheads are taken away and the company is left with its Net Profit, after Interest, but before taxation. When this profit is transferred to the Balance Sheet, it's no longer called Net Profit, it's called Reserves.

The term, Reserves can be misleading because it might cause people to think that this is money that's held back in a *reserve* and stored in a bank vault or something. This is not the case at all, Reserves is simply the Balance Sheet term for Profit.

A company can generate profit or reserves in a number of different ways such as day-to-day trading, the selling of assets, or profit generation that is not within the normal trading activity of the company, such as trading shares on the stock market for instance. Because reserves can be generated in different ways, the Balance Sheet shows these reserves as different categories.

Revenue Reserves

This represents the *accumulated* Net Profit generated from the revenues of normal day-to-day trading activities of the company. i.e. Sales, Service, Parts, Bodyshop, less Overheads.

The accumulated Net Profit means that this is the profit that has been generated and left in the company from the time that the company's life began.

For instance, if a company declared a Net Profit of £20,000 at the end in its first year, the Revenue Reserves on the Balance Sheet would be £20,000.

If the company declares a Net Profit of £30,000 in its second year of trading, the Balance Sheet carries forward the first year's Revenue Reserves and adds the second year's Revenue Reserves to show an accumulated figure. In year 2, the Revenue Reserves would therefore be reported at £50,000.

Remember that this £50,000 in Revenue Reserves is not cash sitting in a bank vault; it's the accumulated Net Profits that have been declared from the previous years of trading and it's already been spent.

Reserves To Date

Balance Sheets are formally prepared on an annual basis, but to have any real value to the Manager, they need to be prepared on a monthly basis so that accurate trend analysis can take place. Where monthly Balance Sheets are constructed, the Reserves To Date represent the Net Profit that has been earned by the company in the current year and will therefore change every month.

At the end of the financial year, the Accountant will make deductions for depreciation and make provisions for other items. The Net Profit that is left will be the declared Net Profit for that financial year. When the formal Balance Sheet for the Year is constructed, the Reserves To Date will be removed and the Net Profit for the year will be added to the Revenue Reserves.

A new financial year will begin and the Reserves To Date will show the first month's Net Profit (or loss). This will continue to accumulate as each month passes. Revenue Reserves show the Net Profit changing on an annual basis and the Reserves To Date show the Net Profit changing on a monthly basis.

Revaluation Reserves

This represents profit that is generated through the revaluation of company assets rather than the normal day-to-day trading activities in Sales, Service Parts and Bodyshop.

When property prices are increasing, the Directors of the company may choose to have the Land and Buildings re-valued to reflect current market values. When the value of the Land and Building increases the Balance Sheet will show a higher value for the Land and Building in the Fixed Assets and the value of uplift will be shown in Revaluation Reserves.

Unlike Revenue Reserves, there is no actual sale or transaction involved in this exercise and therefore no cash is generated. The revaluation process is a paper exercise showing what the profit on the property is likely to be if it were to be sold at its true market value. The purpose of conducting this exercise is to strengthen the owners Equity % to gain additional borrowings in the future.

Capital Reserves

This represents profit or reserves that have been generated from the sale of a Fixed Asset. In other words, when Fixed Assets are sold for more than their stated value, the profit earned from them is classified as a Capital Reserve.

Summary: A company will generate profit in different ways and the Balance Sheet shows these profits as Reserves:

Revenue Reserves:

Accumulated annual Net Profit gathered over the lifetime of the company.

Reserves To Date:

Year to date Net Profit accumulated monthly. This is reset at the beginning of each financial year.

Revaluation Reserves:

Profit earned on the revaluation of property. A paper exercise that does not generate any cash.

Capital Reserves

Profit earned on the sale of Fixed Assets.

Balance Sheet Knowledge Assessment

To reinforce your knowledge, have a pencil, paper and calculator to hand and compile the following components for Insight Motors into a functional Balance Sheet. *(The answer is on page 302)*

Once completed, assess the Balance Sheet to see if the company has sufficient Working Capital to survive. *(The answer is on page 303)*

Insight Motor Balance Sheet Data

Share Capital	50,000
Equipment	146,873
Company Vehicles	92,361
Revenue Reserves	661,254
Bank Overdraft	274,166
Used Vehicles	431,952
Long-term loans	580,000
Loan Repayments	20,000
Demo. Finance	125,000
Demonstrators	149,226
Buildings	600,000
Parts	138,221
WIP	12,882
Stocking loan	200,000
Accruals	12,000
Debtors	88,332
New Vehicles	88,234
Creditors	75,661
Land	250,000

Insight Motors Balance Sheet

Fixed Assets	
Land & Buildings	850,000
Equipment	146,873
Company Vehicles	92,361
Total Fixed Assets	**1,089,234**
Current Assets	
Used Vehicles	431,952
Demonstrators	149,226
Parts	138,221
WIP	12,882
Debtors	88,332
New Vehicles	88,234
Total Current Assets	**908,847**
Total Assets	**1,998,081**
Capital & Reserves	
Share Capital	50,000
Revenue Reserves	661,254
Net Worth	**711,254**
Loan Capital	
Long-term loans	**580,000**
Current Liabilities	
Bank Overdraft	274,166
Loan Repayments	20,000
Demo. Finance	125,000
Stocking loan	200,000
Accruals	12,000
Creditors	75,661
Total Current Liabilities	**706,827**
Total Liabilities	**1,998,081**

Assessing Working Capital for Insight Motors
Maintaining the correct level of Working Capital is critical for survival for all companies and it demands the constant attention of Accountants and Managers. The formula for Working Capital is Current Assets less Current Liabilities therefore the value of Working Capital for Insight Motors is 202,020. By itself, the value doesn't mean anything until it's put into context with the size of the business; this is where Current Ratio comes into play. The formula for Current Ratio is Current Assets divided by Current Liabilities with the benchmarks between 1.25:1 and 1.30:1. *(See The KPI Book)*

Current Ratio for Insight Motors = 1.29:1 which means that the company does have sufficient Working Capital *(202,020 as calculated above)* to continue trading without any problems on a day-to-day basis. In future months, if Current Ratio started to fall below 1.25:1, the company would begin to suffer the effects of cash flow problems and that's where it all begins to go wrong at the operational side of the business.

Current Ratio is the most important key performance indicator to monitor in any business, but more so for the A Industry because cash has a tendency to go out at a faster rate than it comes in. Understanding the Balance Sheet is the key to survival.

"A business can survive for a long time without making a profit, but it cannot survive for a single day without any cash"

- Jeff Smith

Conclusion

"It's not the strongest of the species that survives,
nor the most intelligent, but the one that is
most responsive to change."

- Charles Darwin

CONCLUSION

The only constant is change – an oxymoron that screams out, demanding to be heard and challenging people to sit up and take notice, but people seldom change until they are forced to do so. It's not until a catastrophe strikes that people take notice and adopt new practices for self preservation. Unfortunately, some make the transition too late and their businesses sink like a torpedoed battleship beneath the waves of change.

Survival in business is not about being strong, it's not about being intelligent and it's not about being profitable, all of those things can be wiped out overnight with the entrance of a new paradigm like the Credit Crunch of 2008. Survival in business is about being responsive to change and to ensure that there is sufficient Working Capital to maintain those changes.

This book has been written to help Accountants and Managers to communicate with each other in what are perceived to be different worlds. To understand business trends and the business requirements of the future, discussions surrounding the Balance Sheet and the availability of Working Capital should be commonplace. It's not new paradigms that wipe out businesses, it's resistance to change. Inertia is a weapon of mass destruction.

As trading environments change and evolve, then so too must the structure of Management Accounts evolve to reflect what is happening.

In addition to this, the skills of Accountants and Managers must also evolve or they too will be drowned beneath the waves of change; some taking their companies with them.

Change in trading environments is inevitable, but the desire to respond to change is intentional. Sometimes it's difficult to change, but that doesn't mean that a response is unnecessary. Knowing and not doing is worse than not knowing at all.

Use this book to structure Management Accounts to match with operational performance and to achieve higher levels of communication throughout the team. Involve Managers and Accountants in discussions with issues and problems that are facing the whole company. Be a bearer of the light, break down any Chinese walls that might exist between departments and move forward together in unison. Evolution has taught us that *"There's safety in numbers."*

For some, this simply marks the end of a book. For others, it marks the beginning of a new journey, not one of seeking new horizons, but one of seeing through new eyes to make more use of company resources that already exist.

"It's not the strongest of the species that survives,
nor the most intelligent, but the one that is
most responsive to change."

- Charles Darwin

***"It's not companies who are successful…
It's the people working within them."***

The one problem with this book is that if you lend it out to a friend, you will never get it back! Naturally, you will want to keep your copy to yourself for safe keeping so that you know where to find it at that critical time when you need it most.

You can obtain further copies for other people in your organisation by contacting one of the following:

To order by telephone in the UK:
01384 371432

To order by telephone outside of the UK:
0044 1384 371432

Email:
jeffsmith@askinsight.com

Visit our web site
www.AskInsight.com

Insight Training & Development Ltd
Publications Department (MA)
P. O. Box 1234
Stourbridge
England
DY8 2GE

Profit Builder

Jeff Smith also writes a monthly newsletter called Profit Builder, which is packed with best practice ideas from around the world. You can subscribe to Profit Builder free of charge at www.askinsight.com

Challenge of the month

If you want to ensure that your knowledge is always kept sharp, there's a question posted to the web site each month to keep you on top of the game.

Jeff-Smith.com

This is a blog that hosts ideas posted by other readers on Jeff's materials. Please feel free to add your own thoughts, comments and ideas.

The KPI Book

"The Ultimate Guide to understanding the key performance indicators of your business"

How To
Make More Profit With Your
Service Department

"The ultimate guide to understanding and improving your Operational efficiencies"

Available to order from www.AskInsight.com

What happens if we buy Jeff Smith's books for all of our managers and then they leave us?
What happens if we don't... and they stay?
PROFIT